Do-It-Yourself Decorating
Step-by-Step
Exterior Painting

Meredith® Books
Des Moines, Iowa

Contents

Introduction

Make no mistake about it—painting the exterior of your home is a large and demanding task. In addition to decorating the house, you're also protecting and preserving it from the elements, including sun, rain, and temperature extremes. Keeping exterior walls, wood, and metal surfaces in good condition is essential: Exterior problems eventually become interior problems.

It can be hard to choose colors and finishes with the huge variety that's available today. So turn to the "Ideas and Choices" chapter (page 6) for help making these important decisions.

With such a large-scale project, it's important to plan your work carefully. The "Planning and Preparation" chapter (page 16) explains the hows and whys of good surface preparation.

Every technique you'll need to know is covered in "Painting" (page 52), as well as tips on the most efficient and cost-effective ways to apply exterior finishes for the highest quality results.

Finally, "Natural Wood Finishes" (page 78) deals with stains, varnishes, oils, and preservatives, and explains the uses and benefits of these products, which are improving in quality every year.

On these pages you'll find all you need to know to achieve a long-lasting finish that you'll enjoy for years to come. Good luck with all of your exterior painting projects. We hope this book will make them go as smoothly and efficiently as possible.

Ideas and Choices

In the final analysis, choosing colors and finishes all comes down to personal taste. Although there are no hard-and-fast decorating rules, there *are* some practicality issues you'll want to consider.

Maintaining the character of your home—old or new—is important. Be sure to think about its architecture and style when you choose your colors. If yours is an older home, researching its original finishes and color scheme may be helpful; there may even be restrictions on your choice of colors if it's a registered historic home.

Try to find inspiration from other houses or photographs of homes you've admired. Then factor in the practicality considerations and the information in this chapter as you make your final decisions.

Painting masonry

Clearly, walls are the largest surfaces on a house and are therefore the most dominant parts of the overall appearance of your home. When it comes to choosing colors or finishes, there are a few general guidelines you should observe. Pale colors appear to visually expand surface areas, and darker colors tend to make them appear smaller. Darker colors also don't show dirt as easily, but lighter colors tend to give a more reflective, brighter overall appearance.

Before making final decisions and buying all of your paint, always make some test samples. Experiment both in sunlight and shade. And be sure to consider the other colors or finishes you're using on windows and doors, and whether your choices will complement each other.

◀ Smooth plaster painted white is a safe, practical way to highlight special features and provide a nice backdrop for plants and garden accessories. Selective use in a deck or patio area, for example, will immediately brighten dark, dingy corners, creating a light, airy feel and the impression of more space.

► Textured coatings, such as stucco, and textured paints provide practical, hard-wearing finishes. They also add depth to walls and provide contrast to other kinds of masonry surfaces.

▼ When choosing colors, it's often necessary to complement other elements of the house and yard, such as the garden, architectural features that need highlighting, or in this case, the blending of the smooth plaster color with the natural stone.

▲ Using color on masonry also helps coordinate two different exterior surfaces. Some houses tend to look too "busy" when several types of masonry are combined. But blending them together with color creates a more complete, harmonious look.

Painting wood and metal

All the miscellaneous features on the exterior of a house—such as doors, window frames, gutters, downspouts, and fascia boards—need some sort of finish. Depending on how attractive they are, you can highlight them to accentuate their characteristics or blend them in to camouflage them.

The examples here show some of the possibilities, as well as how to deal with the practical issues of all exterior painting. For example, choosing a paint or natural wood finish that's especially long-lasting has to be balanced against its decorative qualities. There's a wide range of choices available, so think carefully about how they can transform and personalize the look of your home.

◀ ▼ If you're lucky enough to have hardwood windows or doors, they'll naturally stand out from other features on the house. Apart from the fact that they'll outlast softwoods, their appearance, if kept up, actually will improve with age. So choose finishes that are transparent to let the natural beauty of the wood show through.

◀▼ On exteriors that have little or no painted masonry, using bold colors on woodwork does wonders for the appearance of a house. Dark colors, besides hiding dirt, add character and create a homey, lived-in look. The high-gloss finish on both the front door (left) and garage door (below) is easy to keep clean and is durable but still decidedly decorative. The semigloss, opaque stain applied to the windows and frames complements the green doors, making for a simple yet effective coordination of color.

▲ Purely practical items, such as fences and picnic tables, also can be painted to coordinate with the rest of the house and yard. Wood stains and preservatives come in a range of colors to add decorative appeal as well as protection.

Paint finishes

Almost all of the paints and finishes designed for the exterior of a house can be divided into two broad types: water-based and solvent-based.

Water-based paints have grown in popularity over the years, mainly because they're so easy to use and because they're environmentally friendly. Traditional solvent-based paints have long been considered more durable, but they're a bit harder to use and to clean up than their water-based counterparts.

	PRODUCT	SUITABLE SURFACES
PRIMER	Watery, diluted appearance specifically formulated to seal bare surfaces.	Use a primer for masonry. All-purpose primers are available.
PRIMER-UNDERCOAT	A primer and undercoat in one, providing a base for the top coat(s).	Bare wood.
UNDERCOAT	Dull, opaque finish, providing an ideal base for the top coat(s).	Any primed surface.
SMOOTH MASONRY PAINT	Flat to semigloss finishing paint. Majority are water-based.	Most masonry surfaces.
TEXTURED MASONRY PAINT	Textured, "gritty" flat, or semigloss finishing paint. Majority are water-based.	Most masonry surfaces.
TEXTURED FINISHING COATING	Highly textured, thick, paint coating.	Most masonry surfaces.
GLOSS PAINT	Polished, shiny-looking finishing paint.	Any undercoated surface, ideally wood or metal.
METAL FINISHING PAINT	Semigloss or gloss, available in a number of smooth and textured finishes.	Any bare or previously painted metal surfaces except aluminum.
VARNISH	Translucent natural wood finish available in gloss, semigloss, and flat finishes; totally seals surface.	All bare wood. May be applied over most previously stained surfaces.
STAIN	Deep-penetrating natural wood finish. Variety of sheens available.	All bare wood. Darker colors may be applied over previously stained surfaces.
OIL	Penetrating natural wood treatment.	All bare wood, although hardwoods produce the best finishes.
WOOD PRESERVATIVE	Highly penetrating wood preservative.	All bare or previously preserved wood.

Aside from the finishes listed here, some manufacturers produce proprietary paints that require special preparation and application techniques. Always follow the manufacturer's instructions. The chart below gives you all the information you'll need about the most common paint and wood finishes, both water- and solvent-based.

Always read the manufacturer's instructions for each product. There may be slight variations in some categories given in the chart below.

PROS	CONS	APPLICATION METHOD
Excellent sealer, allowing application of more coats of paint. Many also are preservatives.	Use only on bare or unstable surfaces.	Brush.
Easy to use, timesaving, and quick drying.	Only available water-based.	Brush, roller, or conventional or airless sprayer.
Hard-wearing.	Lengthier application procedure compared to primer undercoat.	Brush or roller.
Hard-wearing; most contain fungicide. Greater coverage than textured counterparts.	Shows surface imperfections more clearly than textured finishes.	Brush, roller, or conventional or airless sprayer.
Hides surface imperfections; most contain fungicide.	Poorer coverage compared to smooth masonry paint.	Brush, roller, or conventional sprayer.
Extremely hard-wearing and flexible; hides cracks and surface imperfections.	Very low coverage, and so more expensive to use.	Trowel and float, roller, or conventional sprayer.
Very hard-wearing and decorative. Easy to clean.	Application takes longer than most other paints; careful application is needed for the best finish.	Brush or roller.
Hard-wearing; prevents rust.	Poor finish for large surface areas.	Brush, roller, or aerosol spray.
Very decorative and easy to clean; some contain fungicide.	Not very durable.	Brush.
Hard-wearing. Enhances the grain and features of natural wood.	Difficult to strip or change color once applied, so colors should be chosen carefully.	Brush.
Used mainly as a nourishing preservative; produces a shiny finish.	Regular applications required. Extra care needed when disposing of cloths because some oils are combustible.	Brush and/or cloth (use cloth to remove excess).
Easy to apply; very effective treatment for decay.	Regular applications needed to maintain color.	Brush or conventional or airless sprayer.

Order of work

It's important to apply all exterior finishes in the right order, regardless of the type you're using. The illustrations on these two pages show you what products you'll need for each kind of finish and the order in which they should be applied. Skipping a step not only will affect the look of your final finish, but also will reduce the protection it provides.

MASONRY PAINT ON NEW PLASTER

1 Bare plaster
2 First coat of masonry paint
3 Second coat of masonry paint

MASONRY PAINT ON OLD PLASTER

1 Old, painted masonry surface
2 Fungicide
3 Stabilizing solution/primer
4 First coat of masonry paint
5 Second coat of masonry paint

WATER-BASED vs. SOLVENT-BASED: THE PROS AND CONS

	WATER-BASED	SOLVENT-BASED	COMMENTS
EASE OF APPLICATION	● ● ● ● ●	● ● ●	Water-based tends to be easier to apply, with less brushing out needed.
DRYING TIME	● ● ● ● ●	●	Much quicker drying time between coats with water-based paints.
LOW ODOR	● ● ● ● ●	●	The smell of solvent-based paints can be overpowering. Minimal odor with water-based.
WASHABILITY	● ● ●	● ● ● ● ●	Surfaces painted with solvent-based paints are easiest to clean.
DURABILITY	● ● ●	● ● ● ● ●	Solvent-based are more hard-wearing, although water-based are catching up with improved formulations.
BRUSH MARKS	● ●	● ● ● ●	More evident in water-based, although improving all the time.
COLOR RETENTION	● ● ● ●	● ● ●	White solvent-based (especially) tends to yellow with age.
CLEANING TOOLS	● ● ● ● ●	●	Water-based is easily cleaned with water and mild detergent. Solvent-based paints take longer to clean up.
EASE OF USE	● ● ● ●	●	All health and safety guidelines make water-based products a better choice than their solvent-based counterparts.

SOLVENT-BASED PAINT ON BARE WOOD

1 Bare wood
2 Sealer on bare wood knots
3 Primer or preservative primer
4 Undercoat: two coats recommended
5 Gloss paint

WATER-BASED PAINT ON WOOD

1 Bare wood
2 Sealer on bare wood knots
3 Primer-undercoat
4 Gloss paint: two coats recommended

WOOD STAIN

1 Bare wood
2 Preservative base coat (solvent-based products only)
3 First coat of stain
4 Second coat of stain (third coat may be required for water-based products)

VARNISH

1 Bare wood
2 Preservative base coat
3 First coat of varnish
4 Second coat of varnish

WOOD OIL

1 Bare wood
2 First coat of oil
3 Second coat of oil

METAL FINISHING PAINT

1 Bare or previously painted metal
2 First coat proprietary metal-finishing paint
3 Second coat metal-finishing paint (if necessary)

Planning and Preparation

Exterior painting projects usually are big undertakings, but by using the right tools and materials and working in a logical order, you can minimize the time and effort you'll need to complete the job. Thorough preparation not only makes painting easier, but ensures that your results will look good and protect your home for many years.

Tools

When choosing and buying tools and equipment, always opt for quality over quantity. A few well-chosen, quality tools will be much more useful than cheaper all-in-one tool kits that often contain many things you'll never use.

It's not necessary to buy everything you see pictured here. Instead, build up your tools and equipment gradually. Also, if you'll have limited use for an item, especially an expensive one such as scaffolding or a sprayer, it makes more sense to rent it rather than buy it.

Preparation

Slot-head screwdrivers

Phillips-head screwdrivers

Chisels

Scraper
A broad, rigid blade for removing old paint finishes

Filling knife
A flexible blade helps to push filler into cracks and holes

Putty knife

Tape measure

Chalk line
Marks a long, straight line

Level

Bucket

Sponge

Hammer

Pliers

Lock-joint pliers
Similar to pliers, but has an adjustable, locking head for a better grip

Dusting brush

Wire brush
Removes loose paint when preparing metal

Caulk dispenser
A dispenser that accepts a variety of caulk and sealant tubes

Electric sander
For large areas

Electric hot-air gun
For stripping paint or varnish

Electric drill

Trowel

Float

Hawk

Access

Stepladder

Extension ladder

Scaffolding

Sawhorses and boards
Make a sturdy platform when working up high and they support doors for painting

Protection

Protective gloves
Waterproof, to keep irritants off hands

Goggles
Keeps dust, spray, and chemicals out of eyes

Dust masks
(disposable)

Respirator mask
Protects against very fine dust and fumes

Drop cloth

Painting

Lid opener

Stirring stick

Paint bucket

Paintbrushes

Angled paintbrushes
Ideal for painting window sashes

Varnish brushes

Brush comb

Brush keeper

Roller cage and covers
Different sizes and textures of covers will fit on the same roller cage

Roller tray

Airless sprayer

Airless spray gun

Ladder safety

Painting the exterior of a house almost always involves working on a ladder, so it's especially important to know how to position a ladder correctly and use it safely. Aluminum and other lightweight ladders are lighter, more durable, and easier to set up and use than traditional wooden ladders. For all-purpose use, your best buy is an extension ladder, which consists of two ladders that you can use separately or join together for access to the highest areas around your home.

TOOLS: Ladder, hammer, ladder standoff, roofing attachment

MATERIALS: Pads of cloth, masking tape, board, lath or furring strip, rope, wooden stakes

POSITIONING A LADDER

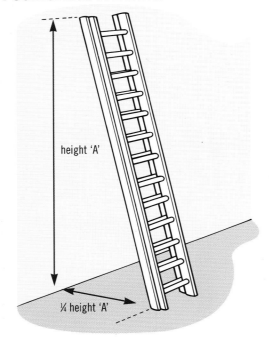

height 'A'

¼ height 'A'

To raise a ladder to an upright position, place it flat on the ground with the bottom feet of the ladder at the base of a wall. Go to the other end of the ladder, pick up the top rung, and hold it above your head. Moving hand over hand, gradually "walk" the ladder into a vertical position against the wall. Now move the bottom feet out from the wall until the distance from the base of the ladder to the bottom of the wall is one quarter of the distance from the bottom of the wall to the top of the ladder. Always maintain this angle at whatever height you use the ladder.

SAFETY CHECKLIST

1 Position the ladder correctly, taking extra precautions on uneven ground.
2 Never overreach: Instead, climb down and move the ladder to a new position.
3 Never climb a ladder so high that your waist is above the top rung.
4 Never rest a ladder on a gutter or downspout.
5 Never leave a ladder unattended.
6 Always try to keep one hand on the ladder.
7 Regularly check the ladder—especially a wooden one—for any damage or wear.
8 Never rush when climbing up or down a ladder.

WALL PROTECTION

To protect wall surfaces during painting, cover the top of the ladder with pads of cloth wrapped with masking tape. Or, buy protective pads for ladders.

SOFT GROUND

Most modern ladders have rubber feet to help the ladder stay put on hard surfaces. On uneven or soft ground, place the base of the ladder on a board and attach a piece of lath or furring strip to further reduce the risk of movement.

EXTRA STABILITY

If the ground you're working on is very soft and spongy, take an extra precaution. Tie one of the bottom rungs of the ladder to two wooden stakes hammered securely into the ground.

USEFUL ATTACHMENTS

Ladder standoff

A standoff makes it easier to work on protruding overhangs or eaves. Commercial ladder stand-offs simply attach to the top two or three rungs, keeping the top of the ladder away from the wall.

Roofing ladder attachments

These attachments bolt onto most modern ladders, enabling you to reach, for example, dormer windows on a pitched roof. The roofing attachment simply hooks over the ridge of the roof, holding the ladder in place while you climb it.

Scaffolding

For the highest areas around your home, scaffolding gives you a safer, sturdier alternative to ladders. Made of strong, lightweight alloy sections that fit together to make a stable working platform, scaffolding is versatile and can be set up to whatever height or size platform you need. Although it's expensive to buy, it's readily available at rental centers.

Always check the integrity of the scaffolding before using it. Older nonalloy types may show signs of rust, which could weaken the structure. Bent or twisted supports or braces also are dangerous. Finally, make sure that all platform components are in good condition.

TOOLS: Level, rope, base plates for uneven ground

1 Although it's quicker and easier to set up scaffolding with two people working together, one person working alone can do the job, too. Always begin by attaching the wheels to the base sections. Make sure that the brake locks are working, and set them on all four wheels before continuing to build the structure.

2 When the bottom sections are all clipped together, use a level to make sure that your base isn't slanted in any direction. On most scaffolding, the wheels incorporate a height adjustment to help with this alignment. On soft ground, always place the wheels on a solid board or plank for extra stability.

3 Always attach stabilizers to the two corners of the tower that are farthest from the wall, and to the other corners, if possible. This minimizes the possibility of the scaffolding tipping away from the wall. If you don't have stabilizers, you can improvise by using sections of ladder tied on with rope.

A TYPICAL SCAFFOLDING TOWER

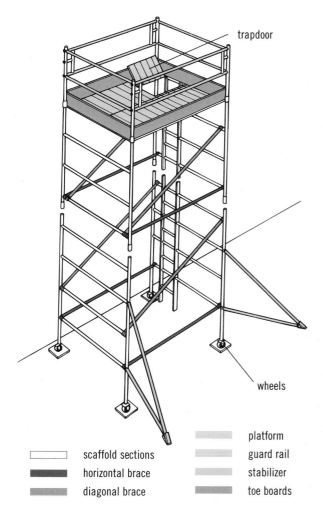

trapdoor

wheels

scaffold sections		platform	
horizontal brace		guard rail	
diagonal brace		stabilizer	
		toe boards	

SCAFFOLD SAFETY

Never stack two short scaffolding towers on top of each other for extra height. Each tower design has a maximum stable height.

Move the tower only when it's fully assembled and on solid, level ground. When the stabilizers are removed, the whole structure becomes top heavy.

Don't leave tools or equipment on the platform while you are moving it.

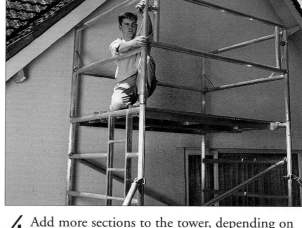

4 Add more sections to the tower, depending on your needs. Always remember to attach guard or safety rails to the top level.

5 Never climb up the outside of the scaffolding; you could tip it over. Many towers have ladders built into the scaffolding sections and a trapdoor platform on the top level. But even if your scaffolding doesn't have these features, always climb up and down from the inside of the tower structure to avoid the possibility of an accident.

Clearing the way

Before you begin painting, you'll need to clear the way by removing any obstacles that might limit your access to the outside walls. Pay special attention to your plants and shrubs; there's nothing more irritating than having to hold a stray branch away from an area you're painting. In fact, if you're working from a ladder, this could be dangerous.

TOOLS: Ladder, garden shears, drop cloth, spade, screwdriver, bucket, lock-joint pliers

1 Use a pair of clippers or garden shears to trim back any plantings or shrubs that are in the way. This is especially important around gutters, where overgrown plantings block the flow of water and even cause leaks. And as any homeowner knows, leaking gutter joints are something to avoid at all costs.

2 If possible, remove the gutters to allow the best possible access to the fascia boards. Some types of plastic guttering comes off easily; simply use a slot-headed screwdriver to gently pry away the clips that hold it in place. With other more common types of gutters, you'll want to leave everything in place and just paint around it (see pages 66–67).

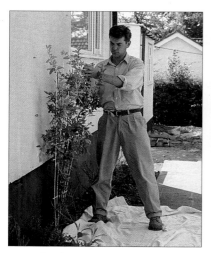

ELECTRICAL SAFETY

Electrical power lines enter many homes at roof height or just below. So needless to say, you must take extra precautions whenever you're working close to such a potential hazard— especially when you're using a ladder. To avoid the risk of electric shock, contact your local power company for its recommended safety procedures before starting any repair or painting work. If you're uneasy working around power lines, hire a professional.

3 Shrubs and plants on trellises up against walls are common obstacles. Wherever possible, remove the trellis supports and gently pull the trellis or shrub forward away from the wall, then lay it on a drop cloth.

4 To avoid damaging the plant, use a bucket to support its weight. Make sure that everything is covered with another drop cloth so your plantings are protected from paint splatters or overspray.

5 Where there's no clear dividing line between the wall and the level of the ground, use a spade to pull back 2 to 4 inches of soil or gravel from the base of the wall. By doing this, you'll avoid getting dirt or grit in your paintbrush, and you'll have a nice, neat paint job at ground level when you finally replace the soil or gravel after your work is done.

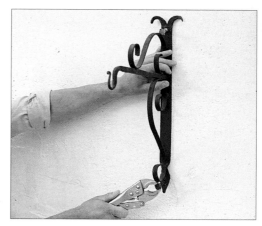

6 If it's at all possible, detach and remove all decorative metal, such as hanging-basket brackets and light fixtures. This will speed your painting by giving you broad wall surfaces that are free of any obstacles, and will make it easier to paint the metal fixtures, too (see pages 76–77).

Types of masonry

When planning to paint a bare masonry wall, you need to first decide whether it's even suitable for a painted finish. Some surfaces accept paint better than others, and some types of masonry would be completely ruined if you tried to paint them.

Shown on these two pages are some of the most common types of masonry that you may have on your house.

SMOOTH STUCCO

HAND-TEXTURED STUCCO

MACHINE-APPLIED STUCCO

A cement-based exterior plaster, traditional stucco must dry thoroughly before it's painted. Stucco finishes may vary from smooth and glassy to textured and rough, but each offers a perfect surface for painting.

Most textured stucco finishes are applied by a trowel and/or a roller and come in various shades and colors. However, that doesn't mean that you can't successfully paint over them after they've become faded or discolored.

Newer, vinyl-based "stucco," spattered onto the wall using a hand-held machine, creates a different type of textured finish. It, too, incorporates its own color but, like other textured finishes, can be painted over if desired.

BRICKS

Common bricks can be painted, but poor paint adhesion sometimes is a problem. The only exception to this rule is glazed-finish brick, which never should be painted.

CINDER BLOCKS

Normally used for internal walls, cinder blocks also are found on small exterior retaining walls. Painting them is frustrating because of their porous surface.

NATURAL STONE

There are many different types of stone, but most usually aren't painted because paint conceals their natural beauty. Also, painting is difficult because the surface often flakes and crumbles.

RECONSTRUCTED STONE

There are many different varieties of reconstructed stone, but all are made from crushed stone molded into easy-to-use blocks. Their natural beauty minimizes the need for paint, but they can be painted if desired.

Identifying masonry problems

Exterior wall surfaces are constantly under attack from the elements. In addition to temperature changes and the destructive properties of water in its various forms, general wear and tear and poor prior paint applications all contribute to the breakdown of a masonry surface. It's important to recognize and fix these problems before you begin to paint. Here are the most common ones you'll find.

EFFLORESCENCE

Caused by mineral salts reacting with water in the masonry and crystallizing on the surface. Scrape away deposits and don't paint the wall until it has completely dried out. When painting over an area that has had efflorescence, use only water-based paints; they'll allow any remaining water or moisture to dry through the painted surface.

LOOSE PLASTER

The plaster layer on a wall sometimes breaks away from its block base, making the wall surface unstable. This is caused mainly by expansion and contraction of water trapped underneath (see Loose Bricks, page 29). Plaster tends to break down in localized areas and always should be removed and patched (see pages 36–37).

RUST STAINS

Caused by external metal fixtures that have corroded and washed down the wall in the rain, resulting in a brownish stain. It also may be caused by old rusting nails or metal fragments below the paint surface that have bled through. To fix it, paint all metal fixtures. Then clean stained areas and seal them with a solvent-based undercoat.

LOOSE BRICKS

Caused by water trapped below the brick surface and expanding and contracting with extreme changes in temperature. This causes the brick to break down. Remove flaky debris and stabilize the area before painting.

MOLD/ALGAE GROWTH

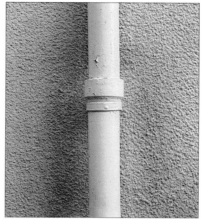

Mold and algae growth is often found in the small damp areas around leaking gutters or downspouts. Once established, mold can become widespread. In any case, it must be treated before painting (see pages 34–35).

CRACKS

Caused by slight movement in the building. If extensive, the cracks should be examined by a professional to check for major problems. Smaller cracks are simply filled with cement or exterior filler (see pages 36–37).

FLAKING PAINT

Caused by poor preparation when the area was last painted or by water penetration. Scrape back to a sound surface before repainting (see pages 34–35).

MORTAR DECAY

Moisture and temperature changes gradually break down the mortar joints between blocks or bricks. Tuckpoint before painting (see pages 74–75).

LICHEN

Like algae, lichen tends to take hold initially in a small area but spreads rapidly. Scrape away all signs of growth and treat the area with fungicide (see pages 34–35).

Identifying wood problems

Wood is even more susceptible than masonry to problems caused by direct sunlight and the devastating effects of water. For example, a window located in direct sun for most of the day is more prone to cracking joints than a window in a dark, damp corner. But in turn, the latter window will be more susceptible to rot and insect infestation. Regular application of the right paints, finishes, and preservatives will prevent these problems from occurring and reduce the risk and expense of having to replace your expensive doors and windows.

DETERIORATING PUTTY

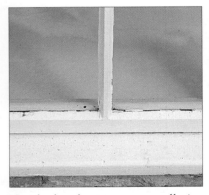

Cracked or loose putty usually is caused by water seeping into a gap behind it, allowed by the slight expansion and contraction of the glass. This, combined with direct sunlight, gradually breaks down the putty and allows deeper water penetration into the wood. Depending on the severity of the problem, reputty or fill the crack (see pages 44–45).

BLEEDING KNOTS

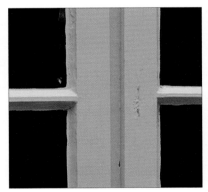

Caused by failure to seal bare knots in the wood before it was primed. Sometimes, even if the knots were sealed, intense sunlight will still cause them to bleed. To fix the problem, scrape away excess sap and seal the area, or use a heat gun to remove any sap remaining in the knot before painting the surface (see page 81).

FLAKING PAINT

Normally caused by aging and constant exposure to sun and rain, or paint that may have been applied over a surface that was ingrained with dirt or grease. Remove all of the flaky material (use a scraper if necessary), then sand the surface and clean it thoroughly before repriming and repainting it (see pages 40–41).

DISCOLORED WOOD

Strong sunlight often will bleach or discolor bare or preserved wood. If the wood will have a natural finish, using a wood cleaner will help restore its color before you apply the new finish (see pages 80–81).

CRACKED JOINTS AND PANELS

Expansion and contraction in wood joints causes cracks that are susceptible to water penetration. Rake out the cracks, then prime and fill them with a flexible filler that will allow for further movement (see pages 42–43).

MOLD/ALGAE

The presence of mold indicates a moisture problem that you'll need to track down and correct before you can do any painting. Wash the area with fungicide and rinse thoroughly.

ROTTEN WOOD

Wood rot is caused by water and by wood-eating pests. In extensive cases, entire sections may need to be replaced. In small areas, cut away loose material and treat and fill the area (see pages 40–41).

Paints and materials

It's always better to buy quality materials; cheaper ones won't offer as much protection. But beyond that, having to apply an extra coat of paint because you bought a low-cost, poor-covering alternative actually can be more expensive than if you'd bought better paint to begin with.

Here are most of the materials you'll need to complete your exterior painting projects. As with tool purchases, be selective. To determine how much paint to buy, see the chart opposite and read product labels.

BASIC SUPPLIES

Sealer
Seals bleeding knots in wood

Powdered filler

Exterior filler

Premixed filler

Flexible filler
For joints and cracks where movement is likely

Wood filler

Stainable filler
For wood that will have a transparent finish

Wood preservative pellets

Wood hardener

Putty
For installing glass in windows

Fungicide
Stops mold growth

Spray-on stain block

Primer/sealer
Seals surfaces before painting

Waterproofing sealant
Clear sealer for bricks

All-purpose cleaner
Cleans surfaces before painting

Steel wool

Sanding block
Sandpaper attached to a support block

Sandpaper
Fine, medium, and coarse grits

Brush cleaner
Cleans both water- and solvent-based paints

Solvent
Thins and cleans solvent-based paints

Masking tape
Prevents paint from getting on windows; helps paint straight lines

Drop cloths

Hand cleaner

Finishing

Primer, Undercoat

Paint, Stain, Varnish, Oil, Preservative

CAUTION
Some materials contain hazardous chemicals. Always read the manufacturer's instructions before using them.

COVERAGE
Try to be as accurate as possible when measuring the surface areas of walls, and treat each wall or surface of the house separately. You can easily measure the width of a wall simply by running a tape measure along its base. To measure the height of a two-story house, pick out a point that's about half the total height, measure to this point, then simply double the figure for the total height.

Use common sense when making deductions for windows and doors. For example, there's no need to worry about making allowances for doors, but the dimensions of large picture windows should be deducted from the overall area.

Estimating accurate surface areas for windows is sometimes difficult. With casement windows that are made up of many small panes and muntins, use the dimensions of the window to obtain an overall surface area. For windows that consist of a pane of glass and little more, make deductions for the glass.

Paint coverages depend greatly on surface porosity. Obviously, unpainted plaster will require much more paint than a wall that was previously painted. So before making a large purchase, buy a small quantity of paint and test it to see how far it goes. Use the chart on this page only as a guide for surfaces of average porosity.

ACRYLIC/WATER-BASED

	sq. yd./gallon
Gloss	82
Primer/undercoat	55
Masonry paint (smooth surface)	65
Masonry paint (rough surface)	22
Wood stain	110

SOLVENT/OIL-BASED

Gloss	92
Primer	110
Undercoat	82
Oil	65
Wood preservative	55
Varnish	87
Wood stain	120

MICROPOROUS PAINTS AND FINISHES
Many products have what are referred to as microporous properties. This means that they allow moisture to evaporate through the finished surface (from underneath) but don't allow it back in (from the outside).

These products have excellent preservative qualities and are especially good for exterior painting and finishing.

However, if you're using microporous products over a finish that doesn't have the same properties (rather than applying them directly to an untreated surface), you won't realize all of the microporous advantages of the new paint or finish.

Masonry preparation

Because walls are the largest surfaces on the outside of a house, they'll use the most paint and will account for your greatest expense. Most masonry paints have a guaranteed life expectancy of up to ten years, but without good surface preparation, that estimate may be cut in half. Surface preparation is worth every bit of the time it takes to do right—and that will depend largely on whether or not your masonry walls were previously painted.

TOOLS: Scraper, 4- to 6-inch brush, goggles, gloves, stiff brush, pressure washer, drop cloths

MATERIALS: Fungicide, stabilizing solution

1 On old or previously painted walls, use a scraper to remove flaking paint or loose material. Anything growing on the walls, such as lichen, also must be completely removed.

2 Check for any signs of mold or algae growth. This most likely will be found on older, previously painted plaster, but also may affect newer unpainted surfaces. Apply fungicide liberally to all affected areas with a large 4- to 6-inch brush. Always check the manufacturer's instructions; the fungicide may need to be diluted before application. Wear safety goggles and gloves.

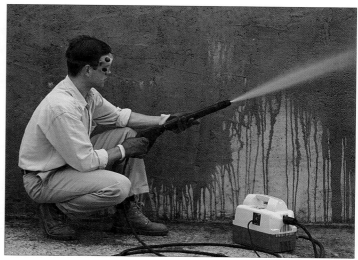

3 On exterior walls that have a thick, extensive growth of mold or algae, it may be necessary to use a stiffer brush if you're going to remove the deposits completely. Scrub the affected areas vigorously. In these cases, you may need to make more than one application of fungicide to clean the surface.

4 You should allow at least 24 hours for the fungicide to kill off all traces of the mold or algae. Then thoroughly wash all areas with clean water. A pressure washer is ideal for this purpose because it cleans off any traces of fungicide and dead algae and removes loose material that you may have missed in Step 1. When using a pressure washer, always remember to wear safety goggles to protect your eyes from flying debris.

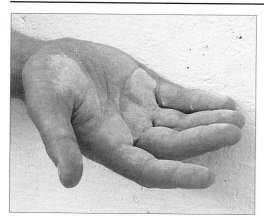

6 These areas should be treated with a stabilizing solution to bind the surface and make it ready to accept paint. Wear protective goggles and gloves, and apply the solution to all affected areas, making sure they're completely covered. The use of stabilizing solution has the added advantage of reducing the porosity of the masonry. That means that your paint will go much further than it would on an untreated surface. Cover all areas with drop cloths, and protect windows and doors because splatters can be hard to remove (see pages 50–51).

5 When they're dry, make sure the walls are sound and free of loose material of any kind. Some surfaces still may have a chalky or powdery texture from mortar or cement breakdown, which is caused by age and general wear and tear.

Patching masonry

It's important to fill all cracks and holes in exterior masonry walls, not just to make a smoother, more attractive surface for painting, but also to prevent water from working its way *inside* your house. Although today's masonry paints will cover and seal hairline cracks, anything larger must be cleaned out and filled. Always use filler specifically designed for exterior use; general all-purpose caulks, fillers, and sealers can't hold up to the harsh effects of weather. Areas larger than about 4 feet square usually require that the entire wall be re-stuccoed by a masonry contractor.

TOOLS: Dusting brush, filling knife, 2-inch brush, sponge, bucket, hawk, plastering float

MATERIALS: Exterior filler, cement, sand, jug of water, mortar plasticizer, household detergent, primer/sealer

SMALL CRACKS

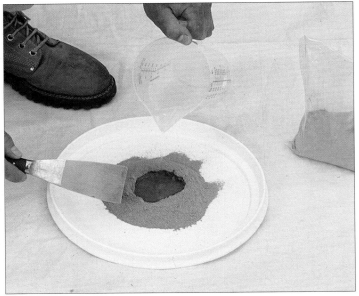

1 The crack must be cleaned of any loose debris, such as small pieces of mortar and grit. A dusting brush can handle most jobs, but if the material is hard to dislodge, you may need a scraper.

2 Pour the required amount of exterior filler onto a suitable surface. Plastic bucket lids work especially well for this purpose because they have a rim to trap water and, because they're made of plastic, they're easy to keep clean. Make a small depression in the center of the filler with a filler knife, and gradually add water, mixing the filler into a wet, pliable consistency.

3 Use a small brush to wet the crack with water. This helps the filler bond with the masonry and slows the drying time, reducing the risk of shrinkage or cracking.

4 Use a filling knife to firmly press the filler into the crack, smoothing the surface as you go. Try to remove any excess filler from around the crack while the filler is still wet.

5 Wipe the filler with a damp sponge. This reduces the need for sanding once it's dry. (Sanding is difficult because exterior filler is coarser and harder than other types.)

LARGE HOLES

1 For larger holes or areas of bad plaster, use a sand-cement mixture for patching. Initially, mix it up dry in a ratio of 5 parts sand to 1 part cement. Add water gradually, and mix to a wet but firm consistency. If needed, add mortar plasticizer to improve the workability of the cement mixture.

2 Remove any loose debris from the hole, and wet the area as covered in Steps 1 and 3 above. A small quantity of primer/sealer mixed with water (1 part to 5 parts water) will help the bonding process between the mix and the wall surface. Transfer the cement mix to a hawk, and use a plastering float to press it into the hole. This is often messy, so hold the hawk below the area you're filling to catch spills.

3 Smooth the surface of the wet plaster, matching it to the surrounding area. Let it dry slightly, then use a wet float to polish the surface. You may need to repeat this step. If the patch starts to bulge, it usually means the hole is too deep to fill in one application. Clean out the patch to below wall level, let it dry, and apply another layer of plaster mix.

Stripping wood

Modern paints have dramatically reduced the need to strip woodwork before repainting it. However, there still will be instances when stripping is necessary. For example, on surfaces covered by many layers of paint, it's often hard to get an acceptably smooth finish unless all previous coats are stripped back to bare wood. Also, if you're planning to use a transparent wood finish such as stain or varnish, all traces of paint will have to be removed. The two best ways to strip paint from wood are with chemical strippers or a hot-air gun.

TOOLS: Hot-air gun, sawhorses, scraper, shavehook, heat shield, old paintbrush, gloves, electric sander

MATERIALS: Chemical stripper, white vinegar, sandpaper, lint-free cloth, solvent, steel wool

HOT-AIR GUN

2 When stripping areas of wood that are close to glass, such as a window frame, attach a heat shield to the nozzle of the gun to keep from cracking the glass.

1 If possible, remove the object to be stripped from its usual position. For example, lay a door flat on sawhorses for easier access to all areas. Hold the nozzle of the hot-air gun approximately 2 inches away from the painted surface. Keep it focused on one area long enough to let the paint melt and bubble, then scrape off the debris using a scraper or a shavehook. Be careful not to hold the nozzle of the gun in one place too long or you could accidentally ignite the paint or scorch the wood.

IDEAL TOOL
A shavehook is handy for stripping because its pointed corners can remove paint from the most intricate areas, such as the corners of window frames.

CHEMICAL STRIPPING

1 Chemical strippers are available in liquid, gel, and paste forms so it's important to read the manufacturer's instructions before using them. The liquid varieties should be applied in a dabbing motion using an old paintbrush. Don't brush out the stripper—it needs to be concentrated and applied thickly to properly react with the paint. Wear protective gloves, and always apply paint strippers with care. They irritate the skin.

2 Let the stripper work for ten minutes to half an hour so it has time to dissolve the paint. Then scrape away the bubbled paint with a shavehook. Don't be surprised if all the paint doesn't come up at once. Some surfaces will need more than one application of stripper.

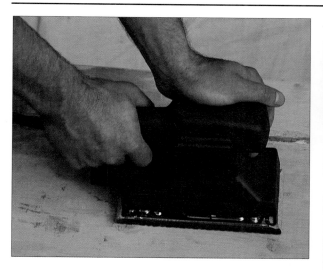

3 When the surface is completely stripped, wash away any remaining stripper with clean water. Or, depending on the type of stripper you used, wash it with white vinegar to neutralize the chemicals in the stripper. Let the area dry, then sand the wood thoroughly for a smooth, clean surface. An electric sander is ideal for large flat surfaces; always sand with the grain of the wood.

4 Finally, remove any dust from the surface by wiping it with a lint-free cloth dampened with a little bit of solvent.

REMOVING INGRAINED PAINT

Paint that's lodged in the grain of the wood can be removed by applying a small amount of chemical stripper to the area and rubbing away the paint with a small pad of steel wool.

Woodwork preparation

By its very nature, wood is less durable than masonry and so requires more frequent maintenance. Even the highest quality paints will rarely last longer than five years on a wood surface, so thorough preparation is important.

General wear and tear, moisture, rot, direct sun, and temperature extremes all take their toll on wood surfaces, gradually breaking them down and making it necessary to repaint. Be sure to correct all of these weather-related problems before you start to paint.

TOOLS: Bucket, sponge, scraper, dusting brush, electric drill, ½-inch paintbrush, gloves

MATERIALS: All-purpose cleaner or household detergent, wood hardener, preservative pellets, filler, sandpaper, primer

ALL SURFACES

Mix a solution of all-purpose cleaner or ordinary household detergent and wash all surfaces thoroughly, whether or not they're damaged. Your goal here is to remove all traces of dirt, grease, and grime. Rinse with clean water.

ROTTEN WOOD

1 Where the wood has rotted in small, localized areas, clean out and fill the damaged spots. With a scraper, cut loose or decaying material back to sound, dry wood. When all rotted wood has been removed, dust away loose debris.

2 Apply wood hardener to the bare wood. This usually is made up by mixing a hardening compound with another chemical solution; follow the manufacturer's instructions carefully. Soak the bare wood with the hardener.

3 As a further precaution to prevent rot from
spreading, preservative pellets may be used.
Drill a series of holes around the rotten area,
spacing them about 3 inches apart. In the example
shown here, it would be a good idea to do this
along the entire length of the windowsill.

4 Push a preservative pellet into each hole.
They'll slowly release a chemical that
impregnates and protects the wood from further
rot. Make sure each pellet rests below the surface of
the wood, then fill and seal the holes with the
appropriate filler (see pages 42–43).

DAMAGED PAINT

1 Repair less severely damaged
areas as well. Where the old
painted surface has blistered or
flaked, simply use a paint scraper
to remove all of the loose or
flaking material.

2 Sand all areas of bare wood
thoroughly, removing any
loose paint or wood. Then
feather the edges of the sound
paint to blend in with the
bare wood.

3 Using a small brush—a
½-inch brush is ideal for
windows—prime the bare patch
of wood, slightly- overlapping the
primer onto the surrounding
painted areas.

Filling wood

Surfaces that have been correctly filled and sanded smooth encourage water to run off—not to pool and cause more structural damage. But just as important, taking the time to fill all of the holes and cracks in wood trim also gives you a much nicer paint job.

Although you'll find a wide variety of different wood fillers on the market, there are basically just two types: those you mix with water or hardeners and then sand smooth when they're dry and those that are flexible enough to ride out slight joint movement.

TOOLS: Filling knife, sanding block, shavehook, dusting brush, filler dispenser

MATERIALS: Powdered filler, sandpaper, wood filler, small spatula, flexible filler, jug of water

POWDERED FILLER

1 All-purpose powdered fillers are ideal for small nicks or holes on the surface of the wood. Pour the amount you need onto a plastic bucket lid and add water slowly, mixing it to a smooth, sturdy consistency.

2 Press the filler firmly into the hole, letting it mound slightly higher than the wood surface. You may need to move the knife across the surface of the filler two or three times to make sure it's securely in place.

3 Let the filler dry, then sand it back to a smooth surface that's flush with the surrounding wood. For slightly deeper holes, you may need to gradually build up layers of filler to get a perfectly smooth patch.

WOOD FILLER

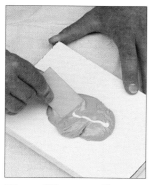

1 For large holes or areas that have been treated for rot, a different kind of wood filler is needed.

These fillers usually come in the form of a thick paste that you need to mix with a hardening compound just before applying them. They tend to dry very quickly, so mix up only what you expect to be able to use right away.

2 Manufacturers usually supply a small spatula for application. Work quickly, pressing the filler firmly into the hole. Again, fill the area slightly high and sand it down when the filler is dry. You'll probably need to make more than one application for a perfectly smooth surface, but the final patch will be very hard and durable.

FLEXIBLE FILLER

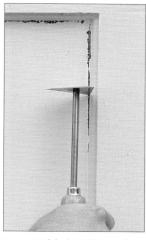

1 As its name implies, flexible filler is ideal for cracks in panels or any area where movement between different parts of a joint is likely. Use a shavehook to rake out loose material from cracked joints, then sand the area smooth. Clean away any debris with a dusting brush. You'll want to do any sanding now because flexible fillers can't be sanded. Apply flexible fillers as your last step—just before you're ready to paint.

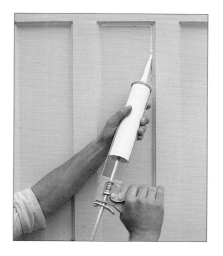

2 Carefully cut off the end of the nozzle of the tube and load it into the dispenser. Hold the nozzle next to the cracked joint and gradually move the nozzle down the crack as you pull the trigger to form a narrow bead of filler down the length of the crack.

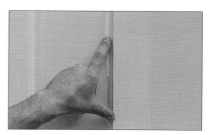

3 Run a wet finger along the bead to smooth the filler and work it into the joint. Now it will be able to ride out minor flexing and movement.

Repairing putty

Putty is the protective barrier that not only holds glass in place in windows but also prevents water from seeping in under the glass and rotting the wood. Putty is damaged by direct sunlight, which cracks its surface, letting water seep in behind the putty and loosening the bond between it and the wood. You can use two repair techniques to fix the problem: Replace badly damaged sections completely or simply fill in minor cracks.

TOOLS: Scraper, dusting brush, ½-inch paintbrush, putty knife, sanding block

MATERIALS: Primer, putty, powdered filler, sandpaper

REPLACING PUTTY SECTIONS

1 Use a scraper to lift out any loose sections of putty. Dust the area thoroughly to remove any remaining dirt or debris.

2 Prime the exposed area of bare wood on the window, and let it dry.

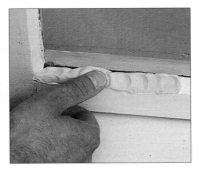

3 Knead a small amount of putty in your hands until it's pliable, then press it into the joint between the glass and wood.

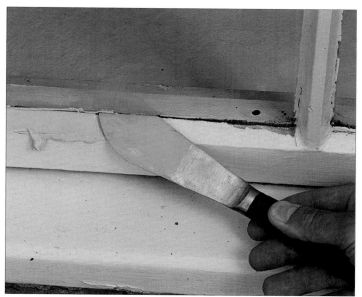

4 Use a putty knife to smooth the putty into position. For a neat finish, keep the straight edge of the knife flush with the glass surface and rest the lower part on the wooden window muntin. This technique takes some practice so don't worry if you don't get a smooth joint the very first time. Remove any excess putty, then let the joint dry completely before you prime the putty.

REPAIRING CRACKS

GLAZING-BEAD REPAIR

Panes of glass also may be held in place by solid wooden glazing beads. These are held in position by small brads or nails. To replace a damaged bead, use an old chisel or a screwdriver to pry up the old bead. Before installing a new bead, be sure to seal the glass-wood joint with clear silicone sealant.

1 If the damaged area of putty is still basically sound and firmly attached to the wood and glass, you can fill small cracks in it with an all-purpose powdered filler. Remove any flaking paint from the putty, sand the surface smooth, and apply the filler with your finger, working it into every small crack.

2 Let the filler dry, then use fine-grit sandpaper to smooth the surface. Be careful not to scratch the edge of the glass with the sandpaper.

Removing broken glass

Although panes of glass sometimes crack when the frame around them expands and contracts, most broken glass is the result of accidents such as stray stones and baseballs. There are obvious safety hazards to look out for whenever you deal with glass, but when carefully done, removing a broken pane is a relatively simple job. Just be sure to keep pets and children away from the area while you're working, and always follow appropriate safety guidelines.

TOOLS: Gloves, goggles, hammer, old chisel, pliers, dusting brush, ½-inch paintbrush

MATERIALS: Cardboard box, masking tape, sandpaper, primer

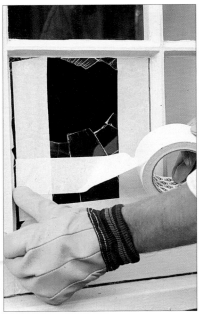

1 First, carefully remove any loose fragments of glass before starting the repair. Wear protective gloves when handling the glass, and keep a cardboard box nearby for the pieces you remove so they won't cut you when you dispose of them.

2 Use masking tape to cover the glass that's still in the window frame. This will help prevent further breakage or shattering while you remove the remaining broken pieces. Attach strips of tape to all areas of the glass, sticking it on firmly.

3 Gently tap the remaining pane with the handle of a hammer. This should loosen the broken glass and make removal much easier. Even though the masking tape should prevent further shattering, always wear safety goggles as a precaution.

4 Once most of the broken glass has been removed, there may be some pieces lodged around the edge of the frame, still held in place by putty. Remove the glass and putty using a hammer and an old chisel, gradually tapping back to the solid wood rail. Again, goggles must be worn for safety.

WINDOW WITH GLAZING BEADS

In cases where the broken pane is retained with solid glazing beads, remove the beads initially using the same method as shown on page 45. Then continue with Steps 2, 3, 6, and 7 below.

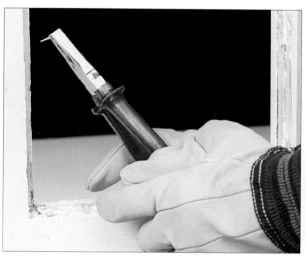

5 Use a pair of pliers to remove any retaining pins or nails from the wooden frame.

6 Sand the window rebate, then clear away any loose material with a dusting brush. Dispose of all the broken glass and debris safely (by sealing it in a sturdy cardboard box, for example).

7 When the window is clear of all loose material, glass particles, and dust, prime the bare wooden rebate with a small brush in preparation for a new pane of glass.

Installing new glass

The most important thing to remember when you install new window glass is the correct thickness of glass to buy. Small windows normally need only ⅛-inch-thick glass, but ¼-inch thickness is more common in larger windows and doors. If the pane was frosted or patterned, take a small sample of the broken glass to your supplier so you can get an exact match.

TOOLS: Tape measure, hammer, putty knife

MATERIALS: Glass, putty, dry powdered filler, glazing points, cardboard

1 Measure the exact width and height of the opening, taking the measurement right up to the muntins. Then deduct ⅛ inch from each dimension to allow for the putty that will be embedded around the glass and to reduce any risk of future cracks caused by minor expansion and contraction. Measure from corner to corner on each side in case the window isn't square.

2 Coat your hands with a small amount of dry powdered filler before you handle the putty to soak up excess oil and make mixing it a bit easier. Take a large amount of putty and work it in your hands. This ensures that the oil and any small lumps are mixed together into a smooth pliable ball.

3 Roll the putty into thin ropes and firmly press them into and around all four sides of the window opening.

4 Carefully place the new pane of glass into the opening, letting the edges of the glass embed themselves into the center of the ropes of putty. Gently press the glass in place by applying pressure at all four corners and along the edges of the pane. Never apply pressure to the center of the pane; it might break.

5 Tap a glazing point into the center of each muntin. They will hold the glass in place while the putty dries and in later years if the putty decays. Don't set the points directly against the glass; you might crack it. Rest a piece of cardboard against the glass to avoid scratching or breaking it.

NEW PANES AND GLAZING BEADS

When replacing an old windowpane on a window that uses glazing beads, measure for the glass as shown in Step 1, but use a silicone sealant to embed the pane of glass into the window frame. Once they're securely back in place with glazing points, the wooden beads will hold the glass in position.

6 Mold more putty into long ropes. While they're still pliable and relatively easy to shape, carefully press them in place over the edges of the glass and up to the muntins.

7 Use a putty knife to smooth the putty into place. The knife is designed to produce a straight, precise line on the glass surface (see pages 44–45). Save excess putty to reuse.

8 Trim excess putty from the inside of the glass using the sharp edge of the putty knife. Let the putty dry for at least two weeks, depending on the weather, before priming and painting.

Masking and covering up

The sole purpose of masking or covering an item is to keep chemicals or paint from splattering on it. Besides using drop cloths to protect the ground, you also may want to mask certain wall areas or wall fixtures. Small drops of paint accidentally splashed on a wooden window isn't a major problem, but it might be on a vinyl window that you didn't intend to repaint.

Although it's always important to mask carefully when spray painting, you won't always need to mask with such precision. For example, at ground level, you can use a temporary masking framework and move it where needed.

TOOLS: Bucket, sponge, hammer, plastic dust sheet, drop cloth

MATERIALS: All-purpose cleaner or household detergent, masking tape, nails, 2 lengths of wood, plastic bag

PRECISE MASKING

1 Before masking a vinyl window, clean it with a solution of all-purpose cleaner or household detergent. Although vinyl doesn't decay or rot, it does need periodic cleaning. The clean surface also will help the masking tape stick and ensure a tight seal.

2 Begin masking by running a band of tape around the edges of the window frame. Use tape that's about ¾ to 1 inch wide; this width is narrow enough to remain flexible when bending it around the edges of the window frame.

3 Use a plastic dust sheet to cover the window, attaching it to the masking tape with another, thicker 2-inch width of tape to hold it securely in place. A clear plastic dust sheet has the advantage of letting light into the house—always nicer than having no window at all.

GENERAL COVERING

1 Measure the width of the largest ground-floor window and the height of the tallest ground-floor window. Add 12 inches to the height, and cut two lengths of 2- to 3-inch-square batten to the extra height and width. Nail the lengths together in a T shape. Don't worry about precision; this is just a rough framework.

2 Drape a drop cloth over the frame and lean it up against the wall so the top of the T rests just above the window. Now you can easily paint the entire area above the window without worrying about getting spatters or overspray on the glass. Move the frame to other ground-floor windows when you're ready to paint them.

3 It's sometimes impossible to remove all fixtures from walls before painting. Objects such as electrical outlets and fixtures can be covered temporarily. Plastic bags are ideal for this purpose. Always make sure that power to the fixture is off when you cover it, or the plastic bag may create a fire hazard.

SUCCESSFUL MASKING

Using tape to mask areas is always a good idea when you want a neat paint job—just remember to remove it before the paint dries completely. If you don't, you risk tearing off areas of the new paint you just applied.

Painting

Now comes the truly fun part of painting—the actual painting itself. Suddenly, you can begin to see the satisfying results of all the hard work you put into surface preparation. But even so, it's important to use the right painting techniques. After all, you don't want your careful preparation work to have been a waste of time. Refer to the Order of Work information on pages 14–15 for the number of coats needed for different surfaces.

Don't start painting if the weather forecast is iffy. Bad weather—even light sprinkles—will not only reduce your paint's protective qualities but it will also ruin its final appearance. On the other hand, painting in direct sunlight speeds drying time and makes the paint harder to spread. Ideally, work on a clear day and try to follow the shade as you paint.

Preparation

As a general rule, start at the top of the house and work down. Fascias and gutters should be painted first, followed by the walls then the windows and doors. Leave any small accessories, such as outside light fixtures and metal trim, until last. First, clean and repaint your gutters before you start to paint the areas below. That way, if it happens to rain in the middle of your paint job, it won't matter if these lower areas get covered in water and debris from the roof; they can be cleaned and prepped when you finish working on the gutters. Plus, paint overspray won't be a problem.

TOOLS: Dusting brush, lid opener, stirring stick, paint bucket, 2 buckets, drop cloth

MATERIALS: Paint, aluminum foil, gauze, large rubber band

PREPARING THE PAINT

1 Before opening the can, use a dusting brush to wipe off the lid; grit and dirt tend to collect around the rim, and debris may fall into the paint when the lid is removed.

2 Pry the lid open with a blunt instrument. You can buy a tool designed just for this purpose and avoid damaging your more expensive screwdrivers, knives, and chisels.

3 Some paints, such as nondrip gloss paints, shouldn't be stirred before use, so always read the manufacturer's instructions. Otherwise, most paints will need thorough stirring. Use either a purchased stirring stick or a length of wooden dowel. As you stir, try to use a lifting motion. This brings up any sediment from the bottom of the can and ensures even pigment distribution.

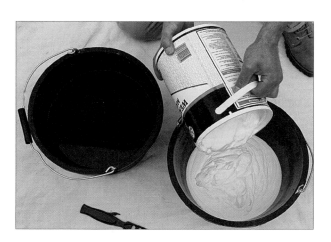

4 It's a good idea to decant the paint into a paint bucket for several reasons. First, the original can will stay cleaner for storage. Second, if an accident occurs, less paint will be spilled. Third, it is dangerous to carry a full, heavy paint can up a ladder, as it may throw you off balance. Finally, if any debris gets into the bucket, it can be cleaned out and the bucket refilled from the original can. Lining a paint bucket with aluminum foil will save time when cleaning it out and switching colors.

5 When using paint left over from a previous job, you may find that a skin has formed. Remove it from the can before attempting to stir. The paint still may have lumps, so it's a good idea to strain it before using it. Put some gauze over the bucket and hold it in place with a large rubber band. Pour the paint slowly into the bucket. You can use this same technique to keep insects and debris from getting back into the main can when you replace the paint at the end of the day.

6 Some manufacturers suggest thinning the paint before application, usually for the first coat on porous masonry surfaces or for practical reasons, such as when you apply it with a sprayer (see pages 60–61). Make sure you use the correct thinner—water for water-based paints or the appropriate solvent for solvent-based paints. Always read the manufacturer's instructions on the can. Use two calibrated buckets for thinning to make sure the thinning ratio is accurate. Stir the thinned paint thoroughly to make sure the mixture is uniform.

Using a roller

Covering large surfaces is quick and easy with a roller, so it's an ideal tool for painting masonry. Rough or textured walls will need a roller cover with a longer nap in order to work the paint into every indentation and hollow. Don't try to make do—buy the right roller cover for the type of surface you'll be painting.

Begin at the top and work your way down. Be sure to cover the ground with drop cloths because there will inevitably be a certain amount of spattering. And mask around any doors or windows that are in your way.

TOOLS: Roller cover, roller cage, roller tray, ladder roller tray, extension pole, battery-operated roller, scissors, drop cloths

MATERIALS: Paint, plastic wrap

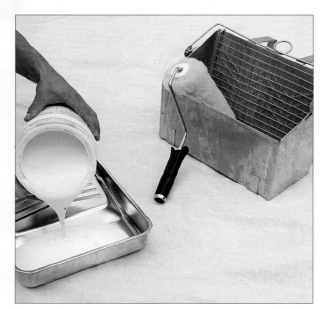

1 A roller tray consists of two parts: the paint reservoir and a ribbed slope to wipe off excess paint and allow it to run back into the reservoir. Pour some paint into the reservoir, filling it just up to the start of the slope. If you're working on a ladder, use a roller tray specially designed to hook onto the ladder rungs.

2 Dip the roller head into the paint and run it up and down the slope to distribute the paint evenly. Be careful not to overload the roller head. Always try to keep the roller tray out of direct sunlight; glare off the paint will attract insects, and heat from the sun will quickly cause a skin to form on the surface.

TEMPORARY STORAGE

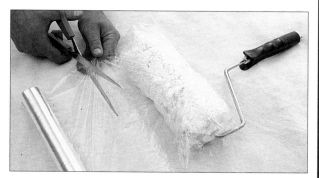

When you need to interrupt your painting—between coats, for example—cut off a short length of plastic wrap and wrap it round the roller head, expelling any trapped air. This will save you from having to clean and dry the roller quite so often.

3 Move the loaded roller over the wall using even strokes. Each time the roller is reloaded, apply it to an unpainted surface, then work back to the previously painted area with overlapping strokes. On rough wall surfaces, you may have to apply a little more pressure to the roller to make sure the paint covers the area completely.

IDEAL TOOLS

Extension pole
Attached to a standard roller handle, an extension lets you paint from ground level areas you wouldn't normally be able to reach. An extension pole also helps your back by reducing the amount of bending you do when reloading the roller or when painting at ground level. Don't use roller extensions when painting from a ladder, though; they take both hands to operate.

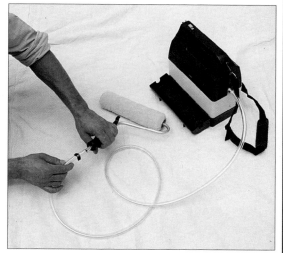

Battery-operated roller
Battery-operated rollers automatically pump paint from an enclosed reservoir to the roller head, eliminating the need to stop painting to reload the roller.

Using a brush

Paintbrushes are the most versatile painting tools you can own. They're manufactured in many different sizes and configurations so it's easy to find the right brush for any painted surface. As a rule of thumb, the more expensive the brush, the longer it will last and the better the painted finish it will produce. Natural-bristle brushes are still your best choice, although good synthetic varieties are available.

TOOLS: Paintbrushes, paint bucket

MATERIALS: Paint, lint-free cloth

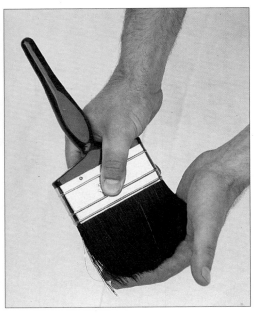

2 Dip the brush into the paint in the bucket so that about one-third of the bristles are immersed. Raise the brush and gently push the bristles against the side of the bucket to remove excess paint. Avoid scraping the bristles against the rim of the bucket; this will build up paint on the bucket's inside edge and leave drips down the outside.

1 Before starting to paint, flick the end of the bristles and wipe them on a lint-free cloth to remove any loose bristles and dust. If possible, use new brushes first to prime wood, or apply an undercoat to get rid of any remaining loose bristles. Then when you use them for finish top coats, their shedding will be done, and you'll get smoother results.

REUSING OLD BRUSHES

Old paintbrushes that haven't been stored correctly may develop bristles that stick out in all directions from the main body of the brush. Although it's possible to trim away stray bristles with scissors so the brush will give a reasonably good finish, it's better to clean and store your brushes properly in the first place (see page 91).

SOLVENT-BASED PAINT

1 When applying solvent-based paint to a large area such as a flush door, begin by painting three vertical parallel stripes, each of which is about 12 inches long.

2 Without reloading the brush, blend the stripes together with horizontal strokes, brushing out the paint to ensure even coverage. Finally, finish off the area with light vertical strokes.

PAINTING A WALL

1 When painting a large area with water-based paint, choose a 4- to 6-inch brush. Use short, alternating horizontal and vertical strokes, applying the loaded brush only to an unpainted area and working back to a painted area. On rough surfaces, a rotating motion may cover the area better.

2 Although rollers cover open areas quickly, it's still necessary to paint around the edges. Brushes are the best tool for this work, which is called "cutting in." The divisions between walls and wood trim may not be as precise on the exterior of a house, so be especially careful in those areas.

3 In awkward recesses, use a smaller brush. Be careful not to overload it when cutting in; this leads to a thick buildup of paint around the edge you're trying to define. Don't worry if you overlap slightly onto a window or frame that's going to be painted; this just makes for a better seal.

Using a sprayer

Using a paint sprayer is a fast, efficient way to paint large surface areas. There are two main types of sprayers available.

A conventional or compressed-air sprayer feeds air from a compressor up a tube into a small reservoir of paint, which usually is located directly below the gun as a self-contained unit. The paint is then mixed with air and sprayed onto a surface by pulling the gun's trigger.

An electric airless spray gun operates by pumping paint under high pressure from a larger reservoir or hopper, up a tube to the gun, then onto the surface. The gun of an airless sprayer is easier to use because the paint reservoir is part of the unit that stays at ground level. For that reason, we show an airless spray gun in use here.

Masking around the area you're painting is absolutely essential whenever you use a sprayer (see pages 50–51). It's also a good idea not to spray in windy weather because overspray travels a long way.

TOOLS: Airless sprayer, goggles, respirator mask, ladder, drop cloths

MATERIALS: Paint, thinning agent (water or solvent), masking tape, plastic dust sheet

1 Sprayers vary in the way they're used so follow the manufacturer's instructions carefully. However, there are some tips that apply to all models. First, make sure the sprayer is turned off at the power outlet. Select the correct nozzle attachment and insert it into the gun. Never point the gun at anyone or put your hand in front of the nozzle. Always make sure the gun lock is on when the sprayer isn't in use, and never try to unclog a nozzle when the sprayer is on.

2 Pour paint into the paint reservoir or hopper up to the level indicated. Some airless spray guns may not have a reservoir; instead, a suction tube is put into a bucket to draw the paint into the pump and the spray gun. Both types of sprayers will give you the same results. The paint you use may need thinning. Make sure it's suitable for spraying: For example, most airless spray guns won't accept texture paint but many compressed-air sprayers will.

3 Turn on the sprayer and adjust the pressure. Test for sufficient pressure by spraying a sample patch.

4 Wear protective goggles and a respirator mask when using a spray gun. Holding the gun 8 to12 inches from the wall, begin at the top and work down, using a constant sweeping motion as shown in the diagram below. Overlap the strips of paint slightly for more even coverage. Never hold the gun in one place; the paint will inevitably start dripping. Apply several thin coats rather than one or two thick coats.

SPRAYING TECHNIQUE

◀ Keep the nozzle about 12 inches away from the surface at all times, and spray parallel to the surface you're covering.

▲ The correct direction of the spray gun across the surface.

5 The versatility of a spray gun really comes into play when cutting in; it even paints the smallest hard-to-reach areas. When you remove the masking tape, you'll be amazed at the neat job.

6 Clean spray equipment thoroughly after each use. This procedure typically consists of filling the hopper with water (or solvent) and pumping it through the system until the spray runs completely clear.

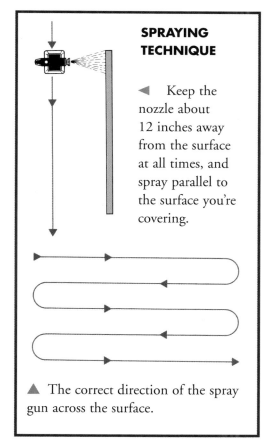

Textured coatings

Coatings with a built-in texture provide a hard-wearing, decorative finish and are becoming increasingly easy to apply to most prepared masonry surfaces. Although they tend to be expensive, they're durable enough to outlast most standard paints. Shop around for exterior plasters, and you'll find a variety of coatings, from traditional, cement-based stucco that you can apply with a trowel, a float, or a roller (and then texture with a variety of special tools) to vinyl-based stucco that is spattered on with a machine.

TOOLS: Hawk, plastering float, 1- to 1½-inch paintbrush, sponge, bucket, textured roller, texture tools

MATERIALS: Textured coating, water

SURFACES AND REQUIREMENTS

Ideally, textured coatings should be applied directly to plaster walls that have been thoroughly prepared (see pages 34–35). Most walls made from facing bricks and blocks also are good candidates, as long as their pointing mortar is flush with the bricks or blocks.

Some manufacturers recommend using a plinth or block for the lowest course next to the ground. Mask around adjacent areas before application (see pages 50–51), and always check the manufacturer's directions before starting to apply a textured coating.

COVERING CRACKS

Textured coatings are great for covering small cracks on plaster surfaces. You can fill larger cracks with the textured coating instead of filler before you apply the top coat.

1 A textured coating may be applied with a roller or, as shown here, a plastering float and a hawk. Applying a textured coating is easier for two people; one applies the coating with the float while the other follows to create the texture.

2 To start, apply a layer that's 1/16 inch thick in an area that's about 1 to 2½ square yards, being careful to smooth the surface and making sure that the coverage is even. Try to finish coating at a natural break in the wall; the finish dries quickly.

3 One way to produce a decorative finish is to run a textured roller across the surface of the coating. Then float more coating onto the adjacent area, and repeat the texturing process, keeping a wet edge on the area you're painting at all times.

4 In awkward or small areas where the roller won't reach, such as cutting in around windows or behind downspouts, dab a small paintbrush in the coating to re-create the textured effect of the roller.

5 There are many different kinds of tools you can use to create a wide variety of textured finishes. Always practice until you can produce a consistent pattern before starting to paint a large wall area.

6 Periodically wash your tools in clean water while you apply the finish. If you don't, the paint will harden in them and begin to slow your work. Finally, remove all masking tape before the coating dries.

Painting a plinth

On some houses, the bottom level of a wall sticks out slightly to form a plinth. This often is painted a dark color to hide dirt that rain splashes up or just to add an extra dimension of decorative appeal. Even if your house doesn't have a plinth, you can create the effect of one by using the technique shown here.

If necessary, before you start to paint, use a spade to remove 2 to 4 inches of soil or gravel from the base of the wall. This will help you avoid getting dirt or grit in the paintbrush and will make a neater finish when you replace the soil after you've finished painting.

TOOLS: Hammer, 2 nails, tape measure, chalk line, level, paintbrush, paint bucket

MATERIALS: Paint, 1- to 2-inch-wide masking tape

1 It's important to make a level, horizontal line for the division between the main wall color and the color of the plinth (or the lower portion of the wall). This is tricky to do if the ground isn't level. To start, use your eye to pick a point on the wall that you think is the right height from the ground. Because there may be obstructions such as downspouts along the wall, you may want to divide the wall into sections. Hammer in a nail at this height close to the corner of the wall, or in this case, next to the natural division created by the downspout.

2 Attach a chalk line to the nail. If you don't have a chalk line, simply use a piece of string and rub some chalk along it. Make sure the chalk color is different from the color of the wall so the line will stand out.

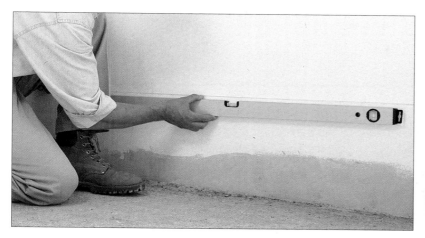

3 Move along to the other end of the wall, holding the string close to the wall surface. Use a level to position the line. This is easier with two people; one holds the string while the other holds the level. Even so, if you take your time and balance the level carefully, you'll find that you can do the job alone. When you're sure that your line is level, hammer in another nail and tie off the string, making sure that it's tight against the wall surface.

4 Now move to the center point of the chalk line and pull it back about 2 or 3 inches from the wall. Then release the line quickly, snapping it on the wall to make a perfectly straight and level guideline.

5 Remove the line and nails, and mask along, and slightly above, the chalk line. Make sure the edges of the masking tape are firmly stuck down so the painted line will be even.

6 Paint the plinth, covering the lower edge of the masking tape without going over the top edge. To make sure that paint doesn't seep under the lower edge of the tape, start your brush strokes on the masking tape, then brush down, away from the tape edge. Brushing in the other direction may force paint under the tape and result in a ragged paint edge.

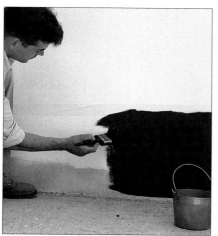

7 When the entire area is painted, remove the masking tape. You should find a neat, level paint division. With one section of the wall done, you'll have a starting level to help you continue the line onto the next wall section or past an obstruction. On rough wall surfaces, it may be impossible to mask successfully. In that case, simply paint the plinth by eye, using a level chalk line as a guide.

Gutters

The sole purpose of gutters is to channel water away from the house. Of all the components on your house, gutters are the ones that must withstand the greatest attack from water. Keeping them in good condition also protects the rest of your house. And, besides their purely practical function, when kept clean and painted, gutters enhance the appearance of your home. There are two main types of gutters: vinyl and metal. Although you may find some gutters made of asbestos, they're usually on historic houses.

TOOLS: Bucket, sponge, sawhorses, filler dispenser, 1- to 2-inch paintbrush, small paintbrush

MATERIALS: Paint, gutter sealant, all-purpose cleaner, piece of cardboard, solvent, cloth

METAL

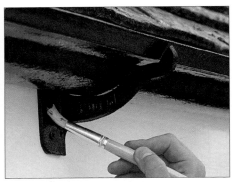

1 Because of their heavy weight and because they're often bolted together and sealed at their joints, cast-iron gutters are almost impossible to remove for painting. Instead, plan to leave these gutters in place and simply paint around them. You'll find that painting the insides of cast-iron gutters will lengthen their life, improve the water runoff, and minimize the chance of loose material building up and causing blockages. Commercial metal paints are suitable for all metal gutters except aluminum.

2 Use a small brush to reach inaccessible areas that you want to paint and protect from the elements. It's also handy for cutting in around the gutter brackets.

3 To avoid splashing paint on a newly painted wall as you paint the backs of your gutter downspouts, always hold a small piece of cardboard against the wall as a paint shield.

ASBESTOS

Because they're now considered a health risk, gutters made of asbestos ideally should be replaced. However, if you decide to repaint asbestos gutters, always wear protective clothing, including a respirator mask. Or, hire a contractor experienced in working with asbestos. Never sand asbestos; the dust you'll create is hazardous. If you have to remove flaking paint, dampen the paint, then carefully remove loose flakes with a scraper.

If you want to paint the gutters with solvent-based gloss paint, prime bare spots with an alkali-resistant primer. Water-based paints are better because you can apply them directly to the asbestos surface and their permeability reduces further paint blistering.

VINYL

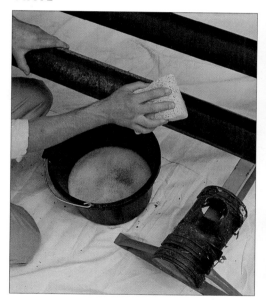

1 Vinyl gutters are fast becoming the most popular type because they're so easy to maintain. Some types even unclip for easy removal and access to fascia boards (see pages 24–25). They're also easy to clean with all-purpose cleaner or a mild detergent solution so repainting is seldom if ever necessary.

2 After many years, sunlight discolors vinyl gutter components. Simply repaint them to restore their brighter original color. No primer is needed; one or two coats of gloss paint applied directly to the cleaned vinyl surface will do the trick.

3 When the gutters are replaced, run some water along them to check for leaks. You'll find that these tend to occur at joints between two sections and usually are the result of a seal having weakened. In problem areas, try to unclip the joint and dry all surfaces thoroughly. Run a bead of gutter sealant around the joint and clip the gutter back together. Immediately remove any excess sealant with a cloth dampened with solvent. Gutter sealant, which is flexible and resists cracking, comes in a variety of colors to match your existing gutters and can be used to waterproof both vinyl and metal joints.

Doors

Exterior doors really take a beating. Sun, rain, and general wear and tear from frequent opening and closing make them good candidates for cracked joints, knocks, and dents. In addition, the front door also serves as a focal point for your house, so it's especially important to give it the best finish you possibly can.

Keep in mind that doors will need repainting often. Take whatever time you need to do the job right and guarantee a painted finish you'll be proud of.

TOOLS: Sawhorses, drop cloths, 1½-inch paintbrush, 2-inch paintbrush

MATERIALS: Paint

PANELED DOORS

1 Front doors usually are more solid than inside doors because they have to stand up to more wear and tear. However, without regular maintenance, they'll eventually deteriorate and will have to be replaced. Pay special attention to concealed areas—such as underneath weatherstripping—where water can seep in and do damage.

2 Before painting the rest of the door, remove it from its hinges and lay it on sawhorses for easier access. Work first on the bottom of the door. Apply a sealer to any knots, if necessary, then a primer-undercoat, and finally a gloss paint. If you use water-based paint, you can prepare, paint, and reinstall a door in a single day.

3 Drips and runs of wet paint are always a problem when you paint vertical surfaces, especially where there are protruding panels or corners that easily collect paint. So, after you've finished painting the door, it's always a good idea to come back and check it regularly as it dries, brushing in any drips or runs that might have formed.

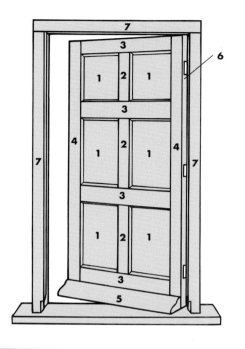

ORDER OF WORK

This diagram shows both the best sequence in which to paint a panel door and the dividing line between the interior and exterior.

1 Panels, working from left to right and downward.
2 Center stiles, from the top down.
3 Members from the top down.
4 Hanging stile, then locking stile.
5 Weatherboard (if present).
6 Hanging edge.
7 Frame.

To gain access to all door edges and to reduce the risk of interruptions due to rain (not to mention the problem of dust and insects getting on your newly painted surface), open the door inward before painting. Remove all accessories, such as handles and door knockers, before painting.

Avoid painting the hinges; the paint will just crack and flake away.

FLUSH DOORS

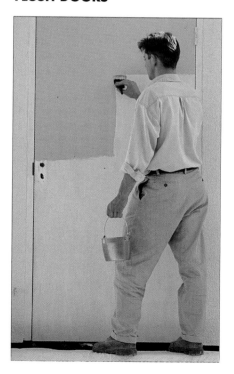

1 Mentally divide the door into eight sections. Begin by painting in the top left-hand corner, then move to the right and down. A 2-inch brush is ideal for this job. Just be especially careful not to overload the wet edges of each section; you'll find this causes unsightly runs and sags.

2 Continue to paint the door, working on one section at a time. Finish the job by painting the door frame and the edges of the door, using a smaller brush.

PRESERVING DOOR SILLS

If wooden door sills are painted, they'll eventually begin to show the inevitable chips and scuffs caused by everyday foot traffic. For this reason, you may want to use a transparent wood stain that's better at concealing wear and tear.

Casement windows

The ever-popular common casement window comes in all shapes and sizes. When painting openable casement windows, it's a good idea to crack them open a bit to make sure that you don't inadvertently "paint them shut." This also will give you the access you need to all of the edges and inside muntins.

Paint casement windows in a logical order; if you don't, you'll find the job nothing less than painstaking. It's also best to paint windows early in the day so they'll have plenty of time to dry before you need to close them in the evening.

TOOLS: 1-inch paintbrush, 1-inch angled paintbrush, paint bucket

MATERIALS: Paint

1 Begin with the smallest opening light, painting the edges and frame rebates. Let the light remain slightly open to avoid sticking.

2 Paint the putty or glazing beads surrounding the windowpanes. A 1-inch angled brush makes it easier to get the paint all the way into the corners of the window frame. Bead the paint up to the glass edge, overlapping very slightly onto the glass to create a sealed edge. Paint the center muntin at the same time.

3 Finish this first opening light by painting the horizontal rails, then the vertical ones. Be careful not to let paint run down to the bottom of the light, making it hard to close later.

4 Repeat this sequence of steps with the large opening casement or light, again making sure that it's not completely closed when you paint it.

METAL AND VINYL WINDOWS

Metal windows that typically are painted are prepared and repainted in exactly the same way as their wooden counterparts. However, if they show any patches of rust, clean them back to sound, bare metal, and treat the areas with a metal primer.

Aluminum and vinyl windows are designed to require little maintenance and so shouldn't be painted. To keep them clean and bright, wash them with warm soapy water. Never use abrasive cleaners on either aluminum or vinyl; they can permanently scratch the surface.

5 Paint the sealed casement. There are no edges to worry about here, so begin with the putty or beads followed by the muntins, and work out to the horizontal and vertical rails.

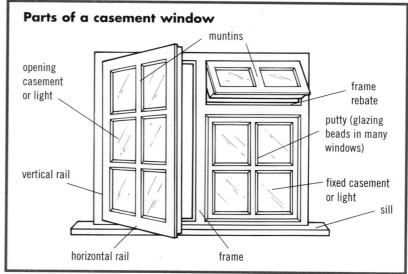

Parts of a casement window

- muntins
- opening casement or light
- frame rebate
- putty (glazing beads in many windows)
- vertical rail
- fixed casement or light
- sill
- horizontal rail
- frame

6 Paint the frame. You may need to fully open the window to do this. Then return it to a cracked-open position.

7 Finish by painting the windowsill, being sure to paint the underside. Most sills have a small groove or drip guard that stretches the length of the underside to prevent water from running back to the wall, where it could seep between the wood and masonry. Always make sure that this groove is free of any obstructions and that there's not too much paint buildup along it, both of which could reduce its effectiveness.

Sash windows

Because of their design, sash windows appear more difficult to paint than they really are. If you follow the right painting sequence, you'll find they're every bit as easy as any other exterior painting job. If the runners are in good shape and you're not changing colors, don't paint them. Too many layers of paint here can make the windows balky. As with all windows, begin painting early in the day so they'll be dry when you close them at night.

TOOLS: 1½- or 2-inch paintbrush, small paintbrush, paint bucket, window guard, window scraper

MATERIALS: Paint

Parts of a sash window

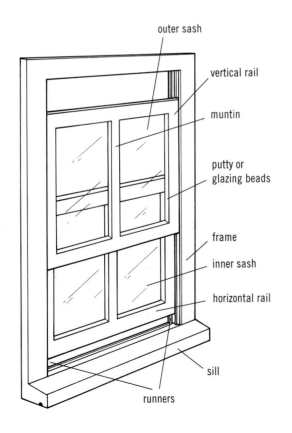

outer sash

vertical rail

muntin

putty or glazing beads

frame

inner sash

horizontal rail

sill

runners

1 Lift the inner sash nearly to the top of the frame, and lower the outer sash about halfway down the frame. Paint the top half of the inner sash, beginning with the putty or glazing beads, followed by the muntin, then the vertical and horizontal rails, including the top edge of the upper horizontal rail. If necessary, paint the top sections of the external runners.

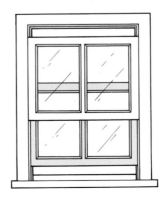

2 Lower the inner sash to a slightly open position, and push the outer sash almost to the top of the window frame. Finish painting the inner sash and begin to paint the outer sash, starting with the putty or glazing beads.

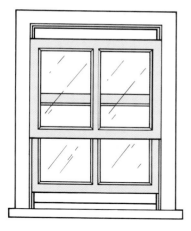

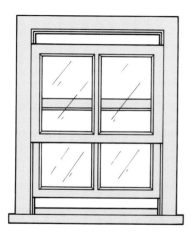

3 Complete the outer sash by painting the muntin and the vertical and horizontal rails, including the bottom edge of the lower horizontal rail. Paint the other half of the exterior runner, if needed.

4 Finish the window by painting the window frame and finally the sill, including the underside, and checking that the drip guard is clear (see Step 7 on page 71).

Parts of a sash window mechanism

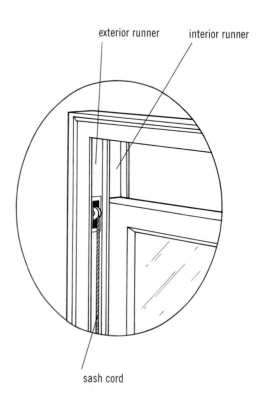

exterior runner

interior runner

sash cord

IDEAL TOOLS

Window guard
Saves time by keeping paint off the glass. Hold the guard tightly against the glass and the rebate, paint around the pane, then move the guard to the next area. Window guards are less effective on older widows where undulating rebates and small joint variations will allow paint to seep under the guard's edges. Clean the guard often to avoid paint buildup and smudging.

Window scraper
Handy for removing dried paint or spray from window glass.

Small brush
Useful for painting runners. It's important to keep paint off the sash cord. If you don't, you'll find the window harder to open and close.

Waterproofing

Although they're not decorative, various waterproofers are essential for routine exterior maintenance and painting preparation. You'll want to call on a professional roofer to deal with flat roofs, but you'll have no problem using clear waterproofing sealant for unpainted walls and flexible sealant to fix any gaps that develop around window and door frames. These products provide valuable protection against water penetration and are especially good for surfaces that are exposed to the elements. Because they're more durable than most paints, you'll be happy to know you won't need to reapply them each time you paint.

TOOLS: Stiff brush, old 2- to 3-inch paintbrush, hawk, trowel, broom, gloves, respirator mask, goggles, filler dispenser, filler knife

MATERIALS: Cement and sand mix, waterproofing sealer, masking tape, frame sealant

WATERPROOFING AND SEALING WALLS

Clear liquid waterproofers don't change the appearance of the surface to which they've been applied. Paint usually can be applied over them if needed (although you may need to wait weeks rather than days before you can apply water-based paints).

2 The quickest and easiest way to remove loose material from exterior walls is simply to use an ordinary household push broom.

1 Surfaces must be filled before waterproofing. Clean out any loose mortar from between bricks and tuckpoint using about 1 part cement to 6 parts sand mix. This mix will vary with the surface you're working on; ask your supplier if it's right for your particular application.

3 Some types of waterproofing sealers are supplied with a trigger spray attachment that you connect to the sealer container. Although this makes it easier to apply the sealer, always be sure to wear protective gloves and a respirator mask. On very porous surfaces, you'll need to apply two coats.

FLAT ROOFS

Older flat roofs, composed of layers of felt and asphalt or coal tar topped with gravel, can develop blisters and leaks. Repairs are best left to professionals who specialize in flat roofs. They may be able to make minor repairs by brushing off the area, *far left,* and applying roofing cement and new building paper, *near left.* More extensive damage needs to be cut away and filled in with a new section of roofing. A newer flat roof may be made of a single ply of synthetic material, such as neoprene, applied like a blanket. These "membrane roofs" are more durable, because they expand and contract as temperatures change. When they need repair, it's also a job for the pros.

FRAME SEALANT

Because of its flexible, rubbery consistency, frame sealant is tricky to apply. For the neatest appearance, you may want to mask around the area you're filling.

These sealants come in a limited range of colors. You can choose one to match your paint or the adjacent masonry.

1 To ensure a neat finish, apply masking tape down each side of the crack. Run the sealant down the crack by applying constant pressure to the trigger of the filler dispenser.

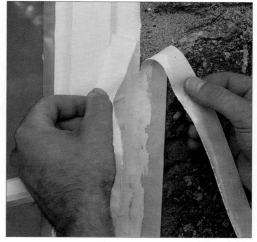

2 If necessary, smooth the bead of sealant with a filler knife that's been moistened with a mild detergent solution. Then immediately remove the masking tape before the sealant cures; otherwise you'll risk disturbing the seal.

Metal

Besides gutters and downspouts (see pages 66–67), there are a number of other metal fixtures commonly found on the outside of a house. Painting these smaller accessories will add much to the appearance of your finished paint job as well as protect and preserve the metal items themselves. Some metal surfaces will need to be treated with special primers before you apply the finish paint. For a long-lasting finish, it's important to use the right products and apply them in the right order.

TOOLS: ½- to 3-inch paintbrushes, wire brush, roller cage, roller cover, roller tray, paint bucket, gloves

MATERIALS: Paint, aerosol paint, metal finishing paint

CAST IRON

1 Before painting ferrous metal such as cast iron, use a wire brush to remove any loose, flaking material.

2 Apply one or two coats of metal finishing paint directly to all bare and previously painted metal surfaces. There's no need to use primers with this kind of finishing paint, so you'll find that you're able to save time and still get all of the benefits of a great-looking protective finish. You may, however, have to use a solvent (instead of water) to clean your brushes and equipment. Always check the manufacturer's instructions for your specific paint.

EASIER PAINTING

It's often easier to take down small metal fixtures for painting. An intricately designed object like a hanging-basket bracket can be painted quickly and easily using aerosol paint. Spray items such as this one on an old board, which serves as a handy nonstick drying surface.

GARAGE DOORS

On large metal surfaces—such as metal garage doors or garden sheds—metal finishing paints aren't your best choice. Although the preservative qualities of these paints are good, it's hard to apply them to large surfaces. The final finish often ends up looking patchy and uneven. It's usually better to use the appropriate metal primer (see below left), then follow with an undercoat and a coat or two of gloss paint. Many metal garage doors come preprimed from the factory.

GALVANIZED METAL

Nonferrous metal surfaces often require a special primer before you can apply the finish paint. For example, galvanized metal has a corrosion-resistant component (such as zinc) deposited on its ferrous surface to give it added protection. When galvanized surfaces need painting, use a primer designed for galvanized metals before you add the finish paint.

METAL MESH

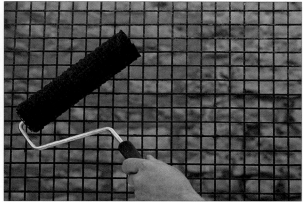

When metal-mesh fencing or trellises need repainting, at first glance, the job may seem practically impossible—at least, if you were to tackle it with a paintbrush. Don't worry. You'll find it will go much quicker if you use a roller. Clean the mesh with a wire brush first, and avoid drips and runs by loading the roller with less paint than you'd use on a wall.

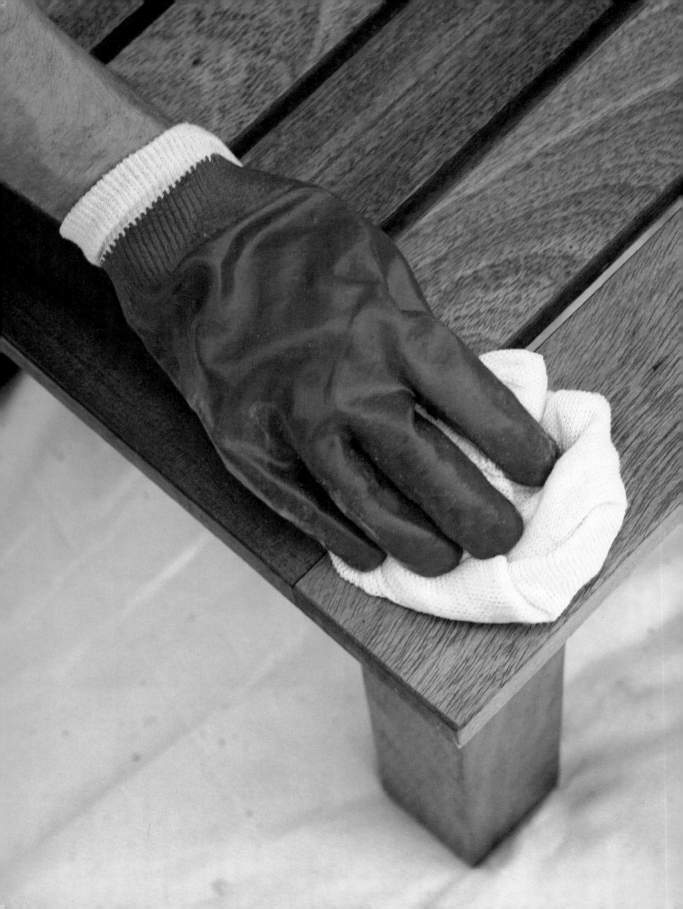

Natural Wood Finishes

There are two options for finishing and preserving wood: to paint it or to apply a more natural-looking finish and let the beautiful grain of the wood show through. Stains, dyes, varnishes, and oils all add an extra dimension to your exterior wood as they protect and preserve it.

Consider using them on more than just your windows and doors. For example, outdoor furniture can be given a natural finish as a counterpoint to a painted house or to help it blend in with a wooded yard. Have fun exploring all the possibilities.

Preparation

If you want to apply a natural wood finish to a surface that's already been painted or to a stained or varnished surface that you want to make a different color, your first step will be to strip the surface back to bare wood (see pages 38–39). You can avoid this time-consuming step, however, if you're just applying a maintenance coat of stain or varnish that's the same color.

When you buy the materials you'll need to prepare your wood surfaces, it's important to remember that your final stained or varnished finish will be mostly transparent. For example, it won't hide wood filler that hasn't been specifically designed to match the wood or finish color.

TOOLS: Scraper, sanding block, dusting brush, small brush, putty knife, hot-air gun

MATERIALS: Stainable filler, sandpaper, lint-free cloth, solvent, protective base coat, stain/varnish, wood cleaner, colored putty

MAINTENANCE COAT

1 First remove any loose, flaky material with a scraper, and fill any cracks or holes with a stainable filler.

2 Working along the grain of the wood, sand back both filled and sound areas until the surface is smooth.

3 Dust off all surfaces and wipe them down with a lint-free cloth dampened with the appropriate solvent.

REPAIRING PUTTY

When repairing putty, use a color that closely matches the existing one; ordinary white putty won't stain well to give you a good match. Ideally, replace all of the putty with glazing beads; they'll last longer. In fact, they're absolutely necessary for varnish: You can't varnish putty.

TREATING KNOTS

Bleeding or seeping knots will ruin the appearance of your wood. Use a hot-air gun to draw the sap out of the wood, scraping away the residue until no more appears. Be careful not to scorch the wood surface; the result will look worse than the bleeding knots you were trying to hide.

4 Touch up bare areas of wood with a protective base coat if necessary (see pages 14–15). Let the base coat dry, then apply the same color of stain or varnish that was used previously. You'll find that the old, sound finish perfectly matches the bare areas that you've just treated. Now the wood surface is ready to accept the top finish coats (see pages 14–15).

REVIVING OLD WOOD

What if the previous wood finish has weathered almost completely away or the wood has become dirty and discolored? Not to worry. You can breathe new life into old wood and prepare it for a more attractive finish. First, treat and fill any rotted areas as you would for painted surfaces (see pages 40–43). This time, though, use a stainable wood filler that's suitable for a natural wood finish. Sand back the surface of the wood to remove any powdery or decaying material, and thoroughly clean it with a commercial wood cleaner.

Wood stains

These versatile and decorative wood treatments come in a wide range of colors. You can use them to accentuate and enhance the wood's natural color or to totally change its color to one you like better. They also come in varying degrees of opacity, which only adds to the variety of effects you can achieve. Although the look of stained wood can be stunning, the best results require a greater amount of effort in comparison to a regular paint job.

TOOLS: Sawhorses, 1½- or 2-inch varnish brush, paint bucket

MATERIALS: Stain, sandpaper, solvent, lint-free cloth

1 Most items have to be stained in position, but doors can be removed from their hinges and stained flat on sawhorses. This avoids drips or runs and makes application easier. Apply a base coat to the wood before staining if that's what's recommended in the manufacturer's instructions.

2 Doors should be stained in the same order they would be painted (see pages 68–69). Always stain in the direction of the grain, brushing the stain well into the surface. Be careful not to overload the brush; this results in a mottled finish with splotchy, uneven coverage.

3 Try to be precise when staining the horizontal and vertical sections of a door and the door panels; overlapping edges of stain and the direction of your brush strokes will show through subsequent coats if you don't thoroughly brush them out in the direction of the grain.

4 Define each section with straight lines, never letting a ragged edge dry or extend onto another section. This would compromise the clear definition of each panel, member, or stile.

5 Use the brush to pick up any drips along the edges. Be careful not to overload the brush, which would make the stain thicker and darker along the corners of the door.

6 Stain tends to raise the grain of the wood, making it slightly rough to the touch. Lightly sand the surface with fine-grit sandpaper between coats, but not after the final coat. After each sanding, remove the dust and fine debris by wiping the surface with a lint-free cloth that you've dampened with a little solvent.

7 The other advantage of taking the door off its hinges is that it lets you get underneath the weatherboard (if present) and stain the bottom of the door. This will protect them from the inevitable penetration of rainwater, which, as we've already shown, can do long-term damage that is expensive to repair (see pages 68–69).

Varnishes and oils

Although stains are becoming the most popular natural wood finish, varnishes and oils are alternatives with their own special qualities.

Varnish is a translucent sealing coat. It's traditionally a high-gloss finish, but less shiny finishes also are available, with color choices growing all the time. Varnish can be applied over most previously stained surfaces and as a maintenance coat when appropriate (see pages 80–83). The main drawback of varnish is that it doesn't last as long as stain and so needs more frequent reapplication.

Oil is a more penetrating and nourishing finish that's especially good for hardwoods such as teak.

TOOLS: Gloves, 1½- or 2-inch varnish brush, paint bucket

MATERIALS: Varnish, oil, lint-free cloth, old can

1 When varnishing bare wood, you may need to apply a protective base coat first. This is especially common with solvent-based varnishes. Some base coats will irritate the skin, so wear protective gloves.

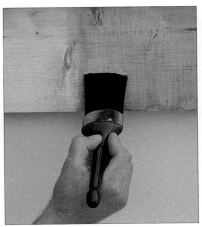

2 If you're using a base coat, let it dry for the time specified by the manufacturer. Then apply the first coat of varnish, initially with vertical up-and-down strokes perpendicular to the grain of the wood.

3 Before the vertical strokes begin to dry, immediately distribute the varnish with horizontal strokes in the direction of the grain. This technique of vertical and horizontal brushing helps ensure complete coverage.

WOOD OILS

Your color choice with oil finishes is more limited. That's because oils act mainly to enhance the wood's original color. Oil should be reapplied every one to two years to keep the wood looking good; fortunately, oil finishes are relatively quick and easy to apply. The preservative qualities of oil last longer than its decorative ones, however, so you can achieve a more weathered, natural look simply by making less frequent reapplications.

1 Apply the oil liberally in the direction of the grain, making sure it saturates the wood. When oiling outdoor furniture, as shown here, turn it over so you can soak the base of each leg to prevent water penetration.

2 Before the oil dries, remove any excess from the surface of the wood by buffing it with a lint-free cloth. This also will polish the surface, giving the wood a light sheen.

3 Oily rags are highly flammable and can spontaneously combust. Don't take chances—place soiled rags in an old can that you've filled with water, then seal the can and dispose of it safely according to your community's guidelines for hazardous wastes.

Preservatives

Applying wood preservative is one of the quickest exterior painting jobs you'll ever do, because so little surface preparation is needed. Usually the wood being treated is rough, and a finely sanded surface isn't necessary. And because most preservatives are applied to large surface areas, you can speed your work by using a larger brush.

Wood preservatives usually are thinner than paints and stains, so there's a tendency for them to drip, run, and spatter during application. Overalls and goggles are your best protection from the inevitable mess. Also, be sure to use drop cloths to protect the adjacent lawn and plantings.

TOOLS: Overalls, stiff brush, drop cloths, goggles, gloves, 3- to 4-inch paintbrush, airless spray gun, bucket, paint bucket, respirator mask

MATERIALS: Wood preservative

FENCES

1 Before coating a wooden fence with a wood preservative, your only major preparation is to use a stiff brush to remove any cobwebs, lichen growth, and loose material (such as dead plants) from the surface of the fence.

2 Apply the preservative liberally so you totally saturate the wood. Because the liquid penetrates deeply into the wood, most runs and drips will simply soak in; your painting and brushing technique isn't critical when it comes to preservatives.

3 If you have to replace an old fence post or are putting up a new fence, soak the bottom of the post(s) in a bucket of preservative overnight. Posts are vulnerable to underground moisture, and this added protection will extend their life.

TRELLISES

A trellis seems to take forever to treat if you use a brush to apply the preservative. The ideal tool is an easy-to-use, handheld airless spray gun, which will cover the area in a fraction of the time. Any material waste will be more than offset by the time you save.

Ideally, remove the trellis so you can treat it where it's most convenient. And be sure to use a drop cloth behind it to protect against overspray.

As always, wear protective clothing, including a respirator mask, gloves, and goggles.

See pages 60 and 61 for more tips on using spraying equipment.

LAWN FURNITURE

1 Make sure the product you've chosen is safe for use on furniture. Keep in mind that the surface of a picnic table is likely to come into contact with food and people, and to be in areas where children regularly play.

2 Pay particular attention to the end grain of the wood; this is where moisture is most likely to penetrate. On bare wood, two or three coats of preservative should be adequate, with maintenance coats applied every one to two years.

Problems and solutions

After your painting is complete, you may find that the finish isn't quite as nice as you'd hoped. There may be various problems that are readily visible or that develop over the first few weeks or months after painting. Most paint problems tend to be small and are relatively easy to correct. More extensive problems usually are the result of using the wrong paint or finish, or not adequately preparing the surface. The most common problems are shown here, along with tips on the best ways to correct them.

GRIT OR INSECTS IN PAINT

Even slight breezes will blow grit or dirt onto fresh painted surfaces. A perfect finish is hard to achieve outside, so you'll probably have to reach a compromise between what's acceptable and what needs further attention. On particularly gritty surfaces, sand back and repaint. Insects also are a problem—they always seem to find their way onto wet paint. Let the paint dry thoroughly, then use a dry cloth or dust brush to clear them from the surface. You'll be surprised how easy this is, and how little damage there is to the paint.

POOR COVERAGE ON MASONRY

The wall surface simply needs another coat of paint. This often occurs when you cover a dark color with a lighter one, or if paint on a rough surface isn't properly applied.

POOR COVERAGE ON WOOD

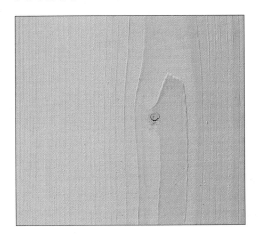

This is caused by applying too few coats of paint or, more seriously, not using a primer on bare wood. Strip the area back to bare wood and prime before repainting correctly.

LIFTING PAINT ON PUTTY

Caused by painting the putty before it was completely dry. Remove flaking paint, let the putty dry completely, and repaint (see pages 44–45).

DRIPS/RUNS

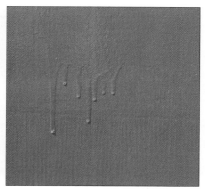

These occur when too much paint was applied to a vertical surface. Let the paint dry completely, sand the area smooth, and repaint.

RAIN DAMAGE

Even a light shower devastates paint that's still drying. Lightly sand small areas and repaint. In severe cases, you may need to strip back to bare wood.

BLISTERING/BUBBLING

This occurs when moisture or air is trapped beneath the paint, (normally on wooden surfaces) and has expanded when warmed by direct sun. Strip back, fill any holes if necessary, and repaint. Bubbling also may be caused by painting directly on top of poorly prepared or dusty surfaces. Again, sand back, prepare the surface correctly, and repaint.

BRUSH MARKS IN STAIN

These usually are caused by poor application. Strip back to bare wood and restain using the correct application method (see pages 82–83). A similar problem occurs if stain is applied on top of a varnished surface; the stain can't soak into the wood and therefore simply sits on top of the varnish. Strip back to bare wood and restain.

ORANGE PEEL/WRINKLING

This occurs when a solvent-based paint was applied over an initial coat that wasn't completely dry. Strip back the area to the bare surface and repaint, allowing adequate drying time between coats. Wrinkling also is commonly found on painted putty surfaces that didn't get sufficient drying time before they were painted over.

Cleanup and storage

Your painting may now be finished, but your work isn't. You still need to clean your equipment and put it away. Please don't make the common (and expensive) mistake of leaving your brushes in a jar of solvent and expecting them to be as good as new when you try to use them again in six months. You'll only find dried-out, ruined equipment. Take the time to properly care for your quality brushes and rollers. You'll be glad you did when you're ready to start your next big painting project. Also remember to safely dispose of empty paint cans and leftover paints and chemicals.

TOOLS: Brush keeper, scraper, brush comb, gloves

MATERIALS: Household detergent, steel wool, solvent, glass jar, clean cloth, brown paper, rubber band, hand cleaner, commercial masonry cleaner

WATER-BASED PAINT

1 Clean roller covers by first wiping off excess paint on an old board or some newspaper. Then wash the cover under running water until the water runs clear. You may want to use a mild household detergent. Rinse and shake dry. If the roller cover was used to paint a rough surface, it probably received a lot of wear and tear and may not be reusable. If that's the case, don't bother to clean it—just throw it out.

2 Wash out brushes using the same technique used for rollers. To remove any dried paint, draw a blunt scraper across the bristles or use a brush comb to loosen the paint. Steel wool is handy for cleaning the ferrule of a brush or a metal roller cage that's become caked with a lot of dried paint.

SOLVENT-BASED PAINT

2 Take out the brush, removing the excess cleaning agent by drawing the bristles across the edge of the jar. Dry the brush thoroughly with a clean

1 Remove any excess paint from the brush and stir it vigorously in a jar of solvent or commercial brush cleaner.

cloth. Repeat Steps 1 and 2 if there's still paint left in the bristles. Finally, wash the brush with warm water and detergent, rinse it, and shake it dry.

BRUSH KEEPER

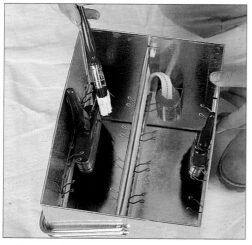

When you're using solvent-based paint on a job that will last several days, you might want to invest in a commercial brush keeper, which you can order from many paint stores. Instead of cleaning brushes at the end of each day, hang same-color brushes in the box, where they're kept moist for their next use.

CLEANING UP PAINT SPOTS

Once your painting is finished and all accessories are back in place, it's not unusual to find that the odd paint splash or run has found its way onto unpainted masonry or ground surfaces.

Fortunately, commercial masonry cleaners are available to clean them up. Simply spray or dab on some of the cleaner and wipe it off with a damp cloth. Wear protective gloves to keep the chemicals off your hands.

STORAGE

All brushes should be dry before they're put away. To keep them in like-new condition, wrap the bristles in brown paper held in place with a rubber band. This will help the brush keep its shape and prevent bristles from splaying out in all directions.

Glossary

Beading
Using the extreme edge of a paintbrush to make a precise dividing line between two colors or surfaces.

Casement window
A window made up of hinged and/or fixed lights.

Chalk line
A length of string covered in chalk dust, pulled tight, and snapped against a surface to leave a straight guideline.

Cutting in
Applying paint into a corner, such as between a wall and the ceiling, or on a narrow surface such as a window muntin.

Dowel
A short, round length of wood (ideal for stirring paint).

Fascia
Lengths of board located just

below the edge of the roof and used for attaching gutters.

Feathering
Blending in uneven paint edges when sanding.

Flush
A term used to describe two level, adjacent surfaces.

Fungicide
A chemical that kills mold or algae.

Glazing beads
Small lengths of wood used to seal around and retain panes of glass. An alternative to putty.

Glazing points
Small metal attachments used to secure a pane of glass or to attach glazing beads.

Hardwoods
Normally found as smooth, planed wood. Very durable and more expensive than softwoods. Most often used for exterior purposes, such as a front door. A common hardwood is oak.

Hawk
A square metal or wooden board with a vertical handle beneath it. Used as a platform for holding plaster, cement, filler, or textured coatings.

Hopper
A paint reservoir on airless spray equipment.

Lath
A length of straight wood, often used as a guideline. May also be called a furring strip.

Laying off
Light brush strokes made in the same direction to eliminate brush marks left on a painted surface.

Lint-free cloth
A cloth, usually made of cotton, that doesn't shed fibers.

Members
Horizontal wooden struts that are part of a paneled door.

Metal finishing paint
A rust-inhibiting paint that requires no primer or undercoat.

Microporous
The property of a paint or stain that allows moisture out but not into the surface of wood.

Primer
Thinned, specially formulated paint that seals and stabilizes a surface before an undercoat is applied.

Rails
The horizontal and vertical struts that are components of all windows.

Rebate
The part of a rail that's perpendicular to the pane of glass.

Sash window
A window in which the opening sections—the sashes—slide up and down vertically within a frame, counterbalanced by weights held on sash cords.

Soffit
A board positioned at right angles to and below the fascia boards, to enclose the roof space.

Softwood
Normally supplied as either smooth or rough-sawn, softwoods are cheaper and less durable than hardwoods. They're used for all sorts of components, both interior or exterior, such as windows and fascia boards. Common softwoods include white fir, pine, and spruce.

Stiles
Vertical struts that are part of a paneled door.

Tooth
A slightly rough surface that's been sanded to provide a better bond for paint.

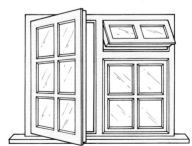

Index

Meredith® Press
An imprint of Meredith® Books

Do-It-Yourself Decorating
Step-by-Step Exterior Painting
Editor, Shelter Books: Denise L. Caringer
Contributing Editor: David A. Kirchner
Contributing Designer: Jeff Harrison
Copy Chief: Angela K. Renkoski

Meredith® Books
Editor in Chief: James D. Blume
Managing Editor: Christopher Cavanaugh
Director, New Product Development: Ray Wolf
Vice President, Retail Sales: Jamie L. Martin

Meredith Publishing Group
President, Publishing Group: Christopher M. Little
Vice President and Publishing Director: John P. Loughlin

Meredith Corporation
Chairman of the Board and Chief Executive Officer: Jack D. Rehm
President and Chief Operating Officer: William T. Kerr
Chairman of the Executive Committee: E. T. Meredith III

First published 1996 by Haynes Publishing
© Haynes Publishing 1996. All rights reserved.

All of us at Meredith® Books are dedicated to providing you with information and ideas you need to enhance your home. We welcome your comments and suggestions about this book on stenciling. Write to us at: Meredith® Books, Do-It-Yourself Editorial Department, RW-206, 1716 Locust St., Des Moines, IA 50309-3023.

This edition published by Meredith Corporation, Des Moines Iowa, 1997
Printed in France
Printing Number and Year: 5 4 3 2 1 00 99 98 97 96
Library of Congress Catalog Card Number: 96-78039
ISBN: 0-696-20677-3